T

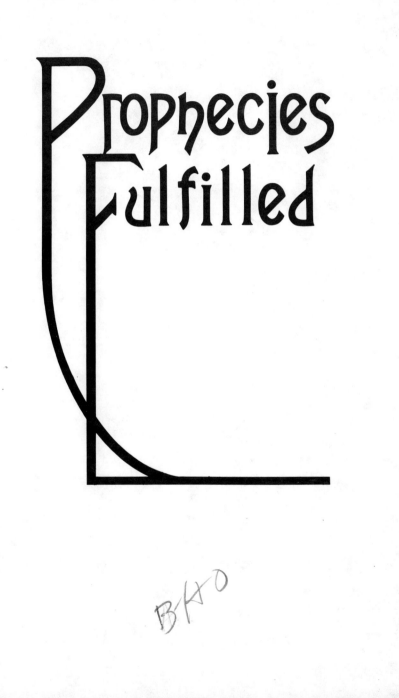

Prophecies Fulfilled

Prophecies Fulfilled

Promises of the Covenant in the Canticles of Luke

Msgr. Charles J. Dollen

Our Sunday Visitor Publishing Division
Our Sunday Visitor, Inc.
Huntington, Indiana 46750

Most Scripture texts in this work are paraphrased or taken from the *New American Bible*, copyright © 1969, 1970 by the Confraternity of Christian Doctrine, Washington, D.C. Brief excerpts from other Bible translations and commentaries are credited in the acknowledgments. If any author or publisher credit was inadvertently omitted, please contact the publisher mentioned below for correction in the next printing.

Our Sunday Visitor Publishing Division
Our Sunday Visitor, Inc.
200 Noll Plaza
Huntington, Indiana 46750

International Standard Book Number: 0-87973-495-7
Library of Congress Catalog Card Number: 87-62881

Cover Design by Steve Windmiller

PRINTED IN THE UNITED STATES OF AMERICA

495

*For B. Gene Hunt,
1935-1986:*

"A true friend . . ."

Table of Contents

Introduction

AMONG the most beautiful of all prayers — treasured in Christian liturgies for as long as they have been recorded — are two canticles or songs in the Gospel of St. Luke: the *Magnificat* (Lk. 1:46-55) and the *Benedictus* (Lk. 1:68-79).

The *Magnificat* is Mary's song of praise as she realizes that all the prophecies of the Old Testament are to be fulfilled through her. It is a magnificent prayer of praise and humility, of faith and gratitude. Through this one song, Mary proves to be a major prophetess of the New Testament.

Zechariah, or Zachary, the father of St. John the Baptizer, introduces the greatest prophet of the two Testaments with his own deeply faith-filled, prophetic canticle of exultation. It reveals the depth of his own longing for the Messiah, and he puts into words the masculine expression of that faith.

For many centuries, the Church has used these two prayers as the high point of evening and morning prayer in the *Divine Office*, now *The Liturgy of the Hours*. Generations of priests and Religious, both brothers and sisters, have had their spirituality nourished by these canticles.

At least since World War I, many of the laity have used these prayers in various translations of the Office or the Little Office of Our Lady as part of their daily devotions. An essential part of the Legion of Mary prayer has always centered on the *Magnificat*.

As part of this ancient and modern Catholic Tradition, this popular exposition of the two canticles is offered to readers to provide a deeper and more complete treatment of some very important verses in the first chapter of St. Luke's Gospel.

9

Section I:
The *Magnificat*

Luke 1:46-55

THEN Mary said:
"My being proclaims the greatness of the Lord,
  my spirit finds joy in God my savior.
For he has looked upon his servant in her lowliness;
  all ages to come shall call me blessed.
God who is mighty has done great things for me,
  holy is his name;
His mercy is from age to age
  on those who fear him.

"He has shown might with his arm;
  he has confused the proud in their inmost thoughts.
He has deposed the mighty from their thrones
  and raised the lowly to high places.
The hungry he has given every good thing,
  while the rich he has sent empty away.
He has upheld Israel his servant,
  ever mindful of his mercy;
Even as he promised our fathers,
  promised Abraham and his descendants forever."

New American Bible (NAB)

11

Prologue:

Luke 1:27

"AND the Virgin's name was Mary."

There is no saint's name so honored by Christians as the name Mary. There is hardly a family of any size but that someone is named for Mary, under that name or a wide variety of modern usages.

We see it in such wide use as Mary, Maria, Marie, Marian, Maureen, and a host of others. Even the various titles and honors accorded the Blessed Virgin Mary are in frequent use.

But the origin of the name escapes the scholars. Here's the way they think it orginated: It probably started with the Egyptian name "Mrjt" meaning "beloved." It was taken into Hebrew as "Miriam" or, better, "Miryam." This was the form used by the sister of Moses and Aaron.

In the Greek and Latin it became "Maria," and finally in the family of English tongues it became just plain "Mary."

Because the Latin root of the name can be translated "bitter," or "sea," the early Church used both in its symbolism.

The "bitterness" was certainly fulfilled in Our Lady of Sorrows, the Virgin Mother of the "Stabat Mater," and other chants of Lent and Passiontide.

St. Bernard, using the figure of the sea, made it famous in his oft-quoted passage on Mary, the Star of the Sea, in his Second Homily on the Missus Est:

"Let us say a few things about this name, which can be

interpreted to mean 'Star of the Sea,' an apt designation for the Virgin Mother.

"She is most beautifully likened to a star, for a star pours forth its light without losing anything of its nature. She gave us her Son without losing anything of her virginity.

The glowing rays of a star take nothing away from its beauty. Neither has the Son taken anything away from His mother's integrity.

"She is that noble star of Jacob, illuminating the whole world, penetrating from the highest heavens to the darkest depths of hell. The warmth of her brilliance shines in the minds of men, encouraging virtue, extinguishing vice. She is that glorious star lighting the way across the vast ocean of life, glowing with merits, guiding by example.

"When you find yourself tossed by the raging storms on the great sea of life, far from the land, keep your eyes fixed on this star to avoid disaster. When the winds of temptation or the rocks of tribulation threaten, look up to the star, call upon Mary!

"When the waves of pride or ambition sweep over you, when the tide of detraction or jealousy runs against you, look up to the star, call upon Mary! When the shipwreck of avarice, anger or lust seems imminent, call upon Mary!

"If the horror of sin overwhelms you or the voice of conscience terrifies you, if the fear of judgment, the abyss of sadness, and the depths of despair clutch your heart, think of Mary! In dangers, difficulties, and doubts, think about Mary, call upon Mary!

"Keep her name on your lips and her love in your heart. Imitate her, and her powerful intercession will surround you. Following her, you will not stray. Praying to her, you will ward off disaster and despair. Meditate about her and you will not err. Cling to her and you cannot fall.

"With her protection there is nothing to fear. Under her

leadership you will succeed. With her encouragement, all is possible.

"Then, some day, you will experience the depth of the meaning in this phrase from St. Luke, 'And the virgin's name was Mary.' . . . In the scintilating light of this star our fervent service of her Son will glow ever more brilliant."

Luke 1:46

1. Text

"Then Mary said: My being proclaims the greatness of the Lord," — *New American Bible* (NAB)

"And Mary said: My soul proclaims the greatness of the Lord," — *The New Jerusalem Bible* (NJB)

"And Mary said, My soul magnifies the Lord;" — *Knox*

"And Mary said 'My soul doth magnify the Lord,' " — *Spender*

"And Mary said: My soul extols the Lord;" — *Kleist-Lilly* (Kleist)

"And Mary said, My soul magnifies the Lord." — *Confraternity of Christian Doctrine* (CCD)

2. Old Testament roots

The roots of Our Lady's spiritual life were firmly rooted in the Old Testament. To delve into the meaning of this prayer means that we must trace its origin to the prayers that she knew and the context of worship with which she was familiar.

This prayer, known by its first word in Latin, *Magnificat*, is a prayer of both adoration and thanksgiving. Every

14

Sabbath, and every time the Holy Family journeyed to Jerusalem, they were reminded of the prophecies, the promises made by Yahweh through the prophets.

Mary and Joseph must have been overwhelmed by the realization that they were caught up in the mystery of the fulfillment of those prophecies. Everything that they longed for, as individuals and as a chosen people, were now being brought to pass. This was "the time" of the Lord.

Obviously, we can only speculate with devotion on Mary's reaction to the Annunciation. After Gabriel left her presence and she had time to meditate on what she had heard, the joy and anticipation must have been tremendous. Could mortal woman be expected to remain silent with such good news in her mind?

Whom would she turn to? Whether or not Ann and Joachim were actually her parents' names, it was most likely, in that particular culture, that she would have turned to them. Of course, it is only speculation that she did, but it is convincing to me.

For a young unmarried girl, a maiden, her trip to visit Elizabeth had to be arranged with parental consent. She would also have needed companionship on the journey to the hill country. That she was properly and judiciously chaperoned on the journey was a necessary presupposition for St. Joseph's trust in her when he was told that she was with child.

And who would have told him? In my opinion, it had to be either Ann or Joachim. After all, the culture in which these people lived was a thoroughly Old Testament culture. There was certainly less change in the customs of the people in a small village like Nazareth than there would have been in Jerusalem. Probably Samuel and David would have been perfectly at home there, as they were in the places of their youth. They were separated by centuries in time but only moments in culture.

15

So, Mary's prayer is an authentic representation of the prayers she knew. In this case, with her soul bursting with the good news, her words would reflect the prayer of Hannah (Anna), the mother of Samuel, when, in fulfillment of her prayers, she was granted a son.

As Hannah prayed, "My heart exults in the Lord" (1 Sam. 2:1-10), we find a source for Mary's words, "My soul magnifies the Lord." Both of these women show their keen appreciation that the good work being initiated is the direct intervention of God Himself. There is no doubt in their minds as to the source of their own joy. This is from God.

There is also an echo of such passages as Is. 61:10, "I rejoice heartily in the Lord, in my God is the joy of my soul."

3. Patristic commentators

St. Basil: Commentary on Isaiah the Prophet
" 'I went in to the prophetess,' he says, 'and she conceived and gave birth to a son.' That Mary was the prophetess, to whom Isaiah drew near in spirit, is clear to those who remember Mary's song, which she also produced under the influence of a prophetic spirit.

"Her words? 'My soul magnifies the Lord and my spirit exults in God, my savior, because He has taken notice of me, His haidmaiden. . . .'

"If we listen carefully to those words, we cannot deny that she was a prophetess. The Spirit of the Lord had come upon her and the power of the most high God had overshadowed her."

St. Bernardine of Siena: Sermon on the Visitation
"The mother and mistress of Wisdom speaks few words, but each is filled with great depths of meaning. We read that the Mother of God spoke seven times, seven

words filled with wisdom, as if to show, mystically, that she is filled with the sevenfold graces.

"Twice she spoke to the angel Gabriel, and twice to Elizabeth. She also spoke to her Son twice, once in the Temple and once at the marriage feast [of Cana]. There she also spoke to the attendants.

"On all these occasions she spoke very little, except for the one time when the praises of God just poured forth from her lips in thanksgiving. Then she said, 'My soul doth magnify the Lord.' But note that here she was speaking to God, not to men."

St. Augustine: Eighteenth Sermon on the Saints
"Now Mary can sing and rejoice in all of her youthful happiness. The joyful choirs of men can join with her in praise. Hear her sing, 'My soul praises the Lord and my spirit rejoices in God my savior. . . .'

"The miraculous new birth has conquered the cause of grief. Mary's song of praise quiets the mourning of Eve."

4. Modern commentators

Abbot Columba Marmion: Fire of Love
"Mary refers to the Lord the glory of the marvels wrought in her. She sings within her heart a canticle full of love and gratitude. With her cousin Elizabeth, she lets the innermost feelings of her heart overflow; she sings the Magnificat which, throughout the centuries, her children will repeat after her in praise of God for having chosen her out of all women.

"Her heart is so in tune with the Holy Spirit that she can sing forth: 'My soul magnifies the Lord and my spirit rejoices in God my savior, because he has regarded the lowliness of his handmaid . . . because he who is mighty has done great things for me.' "

M.E. McIver: "Magnificat" (New Catholic Encyclopedia)

"Mary's song of thanksgiving and praise for the mighty act that God had wrought in her and for the salvation that He had given to Israel is called the Magnificat after the first word of its text in the Latin Vulgate. Although it is the personal song of Mary, it has wider dimensions.

"Set in the scene of the Visitation to her cousin Elizabeth, the Magnificat should be interpreted in the broader context of Luke's infancy narratives. Throughout the first two chapters of his Gospel, Luke presents Mary as the virgin daughter Sion, the personification of Israel.

"Mary is the privileged witness of the events, the object of Yahweh's favor . . . the Ark of the Covenant. The canticles of Luke, ch. 1-2, are songs of thanksgiving on the part of Israel. Mary is the highest and most perfect personification of Israel, the virgin daughter Sion.

"She who found grace with God was the ultimate achievement of the history of the preparation of Israel, the last and summit of the many elections made by Yahweh.

"Mary, then, sings her song as the virgin daughter Sion for all the wonderful works of God wrought in Israel and brought to perfection in the mystery of the Incarnation."

Michael O'Carroll: Theotokos

"The destiny of an individual [Mary] becomes the symbol and the fulfillment of her people's vocation. Identity between Mary and Israel, in its fullness, is implicit in the Magnificat, strongly so as it moves to its final notes — not only the ancient Israel, but the new Israel, which is the Church of God."

O'Carroll says that commentaries on the Magnificat have been constant and fruitful through the ages, from Origen and Ambrose to Luther, Gerson, and St. Lawrence of Brindisi.

5. Meditation

There was no one present with a recorder to take down the exact words that passed between the two great prophetesses of the era that saw the transition from the Old Testament to the New Testament. The scholars will always argue about direct quotations in most of the Bible.

However, the Holy Spirit as the divine author of Holy Scriptures, has us receive these words as the sentiments in the heart of Mary at this time. That should be sufficient to make them our own, as the Church has done in the liturgy for many centuries. St. Benedict attests that this was already in the daily prayer in the Church of Rome in his day.

When we need words to sing the praises of God, when we want to show gratitude for His work of grace in us, we can hardly do better than to use this canticle of Mary. And with all the varieties of translations of that Latin word *magnificat*, I think the most expressive of the sentiments of this prayer are, "My soul magnifies the Lord!"

Luke 1:47

1. Text

"My soul finds joy in God my savior" (NAB)

"And my spirit rejoices in God my Savior" (NJB)

"My spirit has found joy in God, who is my Saviour" (Knox)

"And my spirit hath exulted in God my Saviour" (Spencer)

"And my spirit leaps for joy in God my Savior" (Kleist)

"And my spirit rejoices in God my Savior" (CCD)

19

2. Old Testament themes

Abbot Marmion wrote that joy is the echo of the Christ-life in us. The joy that Mary felt was quite literally because of the Christ living in her, both physically and by faith.

The joy that Hannah felt, as expressed in her prayer (1 Sam. 2), has a martial theme due to her historical context. Israel was surrounded by enemies, and whenever the Israelites won a victory, the whole community rejoiced. "I have swallowed up my enemies; I rejoice in my victory."

Elizabeth must have often likened herself to Hannah, the childless woman, and longed for the same deliverance. As she grew past childbearing age, she probably also likened herself to Abraham's wife Sarah, but without any hope for that type of help.

If Mary had taken something like a "vow of virginity," as presupposed by her answer to Gabriel at the Annunciation, "How can this be since I do not know man?" (Lk. 1:34), then she was also in the position, in fact, of expecting to be childless.

In that sense I like the translation that Kleist gives when he has Mary ready to jump with joy. She must have been very familiar with the psalm verse, "Behold, sons are a gift from the Lord; the fruit of the womb is a reward" (Ps. 127:3). If she indeed had offered to make this sacrifice, then her joy in God's plan was intensely personal.

3. Patristic commentators

St. John Damascene: Third Homily on the Nativity of Mary

"By tracing Joseph's lineage in this way, [Matthew] also demonstrates that Mary, the Mother of God, is from the same line. The Mosaic Law forbade marriage between tribes to protect hereditary land rights.

"There were good reasons to keep the real origin of Christ hidden for a while and to have Joseph take the place of a father, and even to be called by that great title. Legal standing was taken from the paternal line, and this was provided for by Joseph. . . .

"As the Apostle says, 'The husband is the head of the wife.' What is true of the origin of the head is true of the whole body. I think it is abundantly clear that the Evangelist takes such great care to relate Joseph's descent simply to inform us that Mary is of the family of David, the virgin from whom, by an outstanding miracle, was born Christ the Lord, before all the ages, the Son of God."

St. Epiphanius: Sermon on the Praises of the Mother of God

"What shall I tell, or what proclaim, about the excellence of the Holy Virgin? God alone excepted, she is superior to all beings. By nature she is more beautiful than Cherubim and Seraphim and all the angelic hosts. Not all the voices of heaven and earth can praise her sufficiently, not even angelic voices.

"O Blessed Virgin, pure dove and heavenly spouse, Mary, heaven, tabernacle and throne of divinity, you have Christ, the blazing sun of heaven and earth. Brilliant cloud, you have brought Christ down like glowing lightning upon the earth.

"Hail, full of grace, gate of heaven, of whom the prophet sings openly in his canticle, 'An enclosed garden is my sister, my spouse, an enclosed garden, a sealed fountain. . . .' (Song of Songs 4:12)."

St. Leo: Sixth Sermon on the Nativity

"Not only do we remember, we almost seem to see the angel Gabriel presenting his tremendous message to Mary.

We gain some insight into the work of the Holy Spirit, so amazingly promised, so wonderfully believed. . . .

"We are given the form in which we must spread the good news by echoing the heavenly hosts, 'Glory to God in the highest, and on earth peace to men of good will!' The very magnificence of the gift demands that we respond to its splendor with reverent awe."

4. Modern commentators

A. Penna, writing in *A New Catholic Commentary on Holy Scripture*, says that the idea of "savior" as applied to God by the prophet Isaiah correctly interprets how Mary would have used this title in her canticle. God was ready to save His people, even by miraculous deeds, but salvation for Him would be a transforming action, enobling, elevating.

Dom Henry Wansbrough, O.S.B., tells of the difficulties the Judaizers had in translating the notion of savior from Yahweh to Jesus. Paul had many conflicts with the Judaizers, especially in their notion of the necessity of embracing Judaism as a prelude to becoming Christian. With Christ as "savior," the Old Law had to be left behind to embrace the New. This may account for St. Paul's frequent references to Christ *the* Savior in the pastoral epistles.

5. Meditation

The mystery of "The Visitation" contains so many aspects of the Incarnation that it is practically endless in meaning and application. In this verse Mary directs our attention to the joy we should have in this fundamental fact that we have been saved by the actions of God. As we see these actions unfold in history, it is the grace of Christ so freely given to us that "saves and sets us free."

Because we have Christ as Savior, Christian devotion

can then go on and can develop devotion to the Sacred Heart of Jesus, Christ the King and Ruler, Christ the High Priest, and a host of others. Marian devotion kept pace with this historical development of devotion, but it must always be solidly based on the fact of the Incarnation and the role given by God to Mary.

Luke 1:48

1. Text

"For he has looked upon his servant in her lowliness; all ages to come shall call me blessed." (NAB)

"Because he has looked upon the humiliation of his servant. Yes, from now onwards all generations will call me blessed." (NJB)

"Because he has looked graciously upon the lowliness of his handmaid. Behold, from this day forward all generations will count me blessed;" (Knox)

"For he hath looked upon the lowliness of his handmaid; For lo, from now all generations shall call me blessed!" (Spencer)

"How graciously he looked upon his lowly maid! Oh, behold, from this hour onward age after age will call me blessed!" (Kleist)

"Because he has regarded the lowliness of his handmaid; for, behold, henceforth all generations shall call me blessed." (CCD)

2. Old Testament themes

Psalm 113 is a song of praise for the mighty God who

pauses to take pity on the poor and the lowly and have mercy on them. Verse 7 is particularly appropriate: "He raises up the lowly from the dust, from the dunghill he lifts up the poor."

Throughout the Magnificat, Mary shows her awareness of the feminine roles in the Old Testament which were considered role models for the women of Mary's time.

There was the Egyptian maid servant Hagar, the concubine of Abraham who bore him a natural son, only to be cast out after the miraculous intervention which resulted in the birth of Isaac from the true wife, Sarah. Human wisdom had provided the illegitimate son, Ishmael; divine wisdom gave Abraham a true descendant, one of the ancestors of Christ (see Gn. 16, 18, 21). Sarah said, "God has given me cause to laugh, and all who hear of it will laugh with me. Who would have told Abraham . . . that Sarah would nurse children!" (Gn. 21:6-7).

The unnamed wife of Manoah of the tribe of Dan, the mother of Samson, was an example of another barren woman who gave birth after divine intervention (see Jgs. 13). We have already mentioned Hannah, the mother of Samuel at the beginning of the First Book of Samuel.

The story of the handmaiden to the wife of Naaman (see 2 Kgs. 5) also figures in Mary's image of herself as the handmaiden of God, completely submissive to Him. This girl, while unnamed, is still a startling personality, able to speak up with wisdom.

That all generations would call Mary "blessed" started with the Gospel history as recounted in Luke 11:27, which tells of the interchange of the woman who says "Blest is the womb that bore you and the breasts that nursed you," and with our Lord, who elevates it to a higher compliment, "Blest are they who hear the word of God and keep it."

24

3. Patristic commentators

St. Sophronius: On the Assumption

"Truly you are blessed among women because you have turned the curse of Eve into a blessing. You have given hope to Adam, prostrate under the weight of the divine decree. You are indeed blessed among women because the blessing of God the Father has come through you to all mankind, freeing the whole race from the ancient curse.

"Truly you are blessed among women because all your forbears have found their salvation through you, since you are to give birth to the Savior who will open heaven to them. You are indeed blessed among women, because without male seed you will produce the fruit which will fill the world with blessings and destroy the weed of wickedness.

"Truly you are blessed among all women because, while remaining a virgin, you have become the Mother of God. For if the Holy One born of your womb is truly God Incarnate, then you must truly be called the Mother of God, since you have, in absolute truth, brought forth God."

St. Bede the Venerable: Homily on Luke

"Blessed indeed is the Mother of whom it has been said, 'She has given birth to the king who rules Heaven and earth forever.'

" 'But even more blessed,' responds the Lord, 'are those who hear the word of God and act on it.' He graciously acnowledges her praise. He points out that not only is Mary blessed because she gave Him birth according to the flesh, but that she and all others who bring Him forth by good works and nourish Him by their own lives and by sharing their faith with others are blessed.

"Truly the Mother of God is blessed that she gave Him his flesh, but she is by far the most blessed of all in that her love for Him excels for all eternity."

4. Modern commentators

Abbot Columba Marmion, O.S.B.: Christ in His Mysteries

"Consider how the Holy Spirit by the mouth of Elizabeth saluted her on the morrow of the Incarnation, 'Blessed are you among women, and blessed is the fruit of your womb. . . . And blessed are you who have believed because these things shall be accomplished in you that were spoken to you by the Lord.'

"Blessed, for this faith in God's word made the Virgin the Mother of Christ. What simple creature has ever received such praises from the infinite Being?

"Mary refers to the Lord the glory of the marvels wrought in her. She sings within her heart a canticle full of love and gratitude. With her cousin Elizabeth, she lets the innermost feelings of her heart overflow; she sings the Magnificat which, throughout the centuries, her children will repeat after her in praise of God for having chosen her out of all women."

W. J. Harrington: New Catholic Commentary

"Elizabeth has blessed Mary as mother of the Messiah; Mary gives the glory to God in joyful thanksgiving. God has regarded her position as his handmaid, that is, her entire submission to him. The fruit of that submission, that unselfish humility, redounds to the everlasting glory of Mary."

Dorothy Day: On Pilgrimage

"So I am trying to learn to recall my soul like the straying creature it is as it wanders off over and over again during the day, and lift my heart to the Blessed Mother and the saints, since my occupations are the lowly and humble ones, as were theirs."

5. Meditation

Catholic devotion, learned at our mother's knee, has made that title "blessed" a singular part of Marian prayer. She is the Blessed Mother of God, the Blessed Virgin, Blessed Mary ever-virgin, and the ever-blessed Daughter of the Father and Spouse of the Holy Spirit.

Mary is blessed in that she is the First Christian and the Mother of Christians. True devotion to Mary always leads to a deeper understanding of the Incarnation, that Jesus Christ is the Son of God and the Son of Man. True God of True God, but surely He has a human nature which He received from Mary.

We call her "blessed" out of a spirit of wonder and awe, humility and gratitude. That title comes so easily to our lips.

Luke 1:49

1. Text

"God who is mighty has done great things for me, holy is his name." (NAB)

"For the Almighty has done great things for me. Holy is his name," (NJB)

"Because he who is mighty, he whose name is holy, has wrought for me his wonders." (Knox)

"For to me the Almighty hath done wonders, and holy is his name." (Spencer)

"How sublime is what he has done for me — the Mighty One, whose name is 'Holy'!" (Kleist)

"Because he who is mighty has done great things for me, and holy is his name." (CCD)

2. Old Testament themes

The Psalms frequently carry the theme of rejoicing in the God who worked such wonders for the people, as well as for individuals. In Psalm 111:9 we read, "He has sent deliverance to his people; he has ratified his covenant forever, holy and awesome is his name."

Most of the psalms that treat of the history of salvation carry this familiar theme, that the Almighty has stepped into history over and over again to deliver His people, as evidence of both His power and His holiness. Mary would have been very familiar with this theme.

In the call of Moses, Ex 3:41ff., the holiness of God is seen in the burning-bush incident, where Moses is told that even the ground around the apparition is holy.

Even before that, the story of the birth of the twelve patriarchs, the fathers of the twelve tribes of Israel, in Genesis 30 would have been familiar to Mary, and the names of the twelve, especially Asher, proclaimed how "fortunate" the mother was.

Mary would also have felt a special kinship with Ruth, Judith, and Esther. Naomi and her daughter-in-law Ruth are classical examples of how God's ordinary providence works for the good of the individual and is effective to show God's wonders.

Judith's hymn, chapter 16 of the book named for her, contains such verses as "A new hymn will I sing to my God. O Lord, great are you and glorious, wonderful in power and unsurpassable" (v. 13) and "But to those who fear you, you are very merciful" (v. 15). This is in the same family of prayers that Mary was using in the Magnificat.

It can be seen in Esther, F:6 "The LORD saved his people and delivered us from all these evils. God worked signs and wonders, such as have not occurred among the nations."

28

3. Patristic Commentators

St. Augustine: Eighteenth Sermon on the Saints

"Dearly beloved: That long-desired day has come, the birthday of the venerable and blessed ever-virgin Mary, on whose feast the whole world rejoices and exults. She is the flower of the field from whom comes that most precious lily of the valley.

"At her birth, the nature of our first parents was restored and their guilt destroyed. The unhappy legacy of Eve, 'In sorrow shall you bear your children,' is ended in Mary, for she gave birth to the Lord in joy.

"Eve mourned, but Mary exulted. Eve carried tears in her womb; Mary carried joy. Eve gave birth to a sinner; Mary gave us the innocent one. The mother of our race brought punishment to mankind; the mother of Our Lord brought salvation to mankind.

"From Eve came sin; from Mary, grace. Eve was the source of death; Mary was the source of Life. One hurt us, the other helped us. The faith and obedience of Mary compensates for the pride and disobedience of Eve.

"Now Mary can sing and rejoice in all of her youthful happiness. The joyful choirs of men can join with her in praise. Hear her sing, 'My soul praises the Lord and my spirit rejoices in God my Savior. He has had regard for the humility of His handmaiden. From now on, all generations shall call me blessed. Because He who is powerful has done great things for me.'

"The miraculous new birth has conquered the cause of grief. Mary's song of praise quiets the mourning of Eve."

St. Jerome: On the Assumption

"When the angel cried, 'Hail, full of grace, the Lord is with you; you are blessed among women!' he told us by divine command how tremendous was the dignity and the beauty of the ever-virgin Mary. How well we can understand that she would be 'full of grace,' this virgin who glorified God and gave Our Lord to mankind, who poured out peace upon the earth by giving hope to the gentiles, protection against temptation, purpose of life and reason for sacrifice.

"Others may grow in grace, day by day, but in Mary there has been poured the fullness of grace. Although we may know that the holy patriarchs and prophets had grace, it was much different from the fullness of grace found in Mary, the fullness of the grace of Christ.

"When we read 'You are blessed among women,' we understand, 'You are more blessed than any woman ever created.' Whatever penalty was decreed against Eve is totally removed in the blessing poured forth in Mary.

"Solomon sings her praises in his canticle, 'Come my dove, my immaculate one, for winter is over, the rains have come and gone.'. . .

"Jeremiah affirms that she carried a man in her womb without physical contact. He tells us that the Lord has done something unique on the earth when this woman shall bear a man. It is so truly unique that it can have no equal. God, whom the whole world cannot contain, nor any man see and still live, God has found a welcome in her womb. Without injuring her physical virginity, the whole God enters in, and likewise is born, although, as Ezekiel testifies, the door remained entirely closed.

"Solomon goes on in his canticle, 'an enclosed garden, a sealed fountain, your flowers a paradise.' What a garden of delights in which are found all the blossoms and the scent of all the virtues! This garden is so protected that no evil or corruption can enter. This fountain is surely sealed with the mark of the whole Trinity."

St. John Damascene: On the True Faith
    "Mary was born in Joachim's house, near the pool Pro-

batica, and from there she was presented in the Temple. Then, established in the house of God, strengthened by the Holy Spirit, like a fruitful olive branch, she brought forth all the virtues worthy of the household of God.

"The desires of the world and the concupiscence of the flesh never touched her pure soul. She was preserved virginal, both body and soul, as became one who would someday receive God into her bosom."

4. Modern use

Speaking of the wonders that God had accomplished in Mary's soul, Cardinal John Henry Newman wrote two sermons in his collection *Discourses Addressed to Mixed Congregations* on the "Glories of Mary" and on "The Fitness of the Glories of Mary." Here is an excerpt from the second of these two powerful sermons:

"I will state what the Church has taught and defined from the first ages concerning the Blessed Virgin and then you will see how naturally the devotion her children show her, and the praises with which they honor her, follow from it.

"Now as you know, it has been held from the first, and defined from an early age, that Mary is the Mother of God. She is not merely the mother of our Lord's manhood, or of our Lord's body, but she is to be considered the Mother of the Word Himself, the Word Incarnate. God, in the Person of the Word, the Second Person of the All-Glorious Trinity, humbled Himself to become her Son. As the Church sings [in the *Te Deum*], 'You did not disdain the virgin's womb.'

"He took the substance of His human flesh from her, and clothed in it He lay within her; and He bore it about with Him after birth, as a sort of badge and witness that He, though God, was hers. He was nursed and tended by her; He was suckled by her; He lay in her arms. As time went by, He ministered to her, and obeyed her, He lived with her for thirty years in one house with only the saintly Joseph to share it with Him.

"She was the witness of His growth, of His joys, of His sorrows, of His prayers; she was blessed with His smile, with the touch of His hand, with the whisper of His affection, with the expression of His thoughts and feelings for that length of time.

"Now, my Brethren, what ought she to be, what is it *becoming* that she should be, who was so favored?"

Archbishop Fulton Sheen: Wisdom for Welfare, Preface
"In the streets of the Roman world, of which Israel was but a conquered part, there stands an exultant woman proclaiming to all the world the tidings of her emancipation. "He that is mighty has done great things for me." It was a representative voice, not only of Israel, but of womanhood and the world. It was the clarion call of a long-repressed sex claiming its right and hailing its emancipation. . . .

"Not in her times alone, but in her for all times, woman would find her glory and her honor. They could not call her Jew nor Greek nor Roman; not successful nor beautiful but "blessed," that is, holy. And blessed she is because by giving birth to the God-Man she broke down the trammels of nationality and race. Her Son was cosmopolitan. He is MAN *par excellence*. And she is THE WOMAN because she is the Mother of God."

5. Meditation

God who is mighty has done great things for her. He, the Creator, has taken her, the creature, and brought her into the very heart of the economy of salvation. St. Bernard asks the (rhetorical) question — "What if she had said no to Gabriel?"

After all, she is a woman; she has free will; she could

have simply said 'No!' Thank God it is only a rhetorical question, since Mary's will was so in tune with the Divine Will that she wouldn't even have considered a negative answer.

But with her *Fiat!* she did change the course of history. At that instant the mystery of the Incarnation occurred and the Son of God became man. And holy is His name, indeed!

Luke 1:50

1. Text

"His mercy is from age to age on those who fear him." (NAB)

"And his faithful love extends after age to those who fear him." (NJB)

"He has mercy upon those who fear him, from generation to generation." (Knox)

"And his mercy reacheth unto generations upon generations to those who fear Him." (Spencer)

"From age to age he visits those who worship him in reverence." (Kleist)

"And for generation upon generation is his mercy to those who fear him." (CCD)

2. Old Testament themes

The theme of God's mercy runs throughout the psalms and the prophets, all of which would be familiar to Mary. Thus, Psalm 103: "As a father has compassion on his children, so the LORD has compassion on those who fear him" (v.13) and "But the kindness of the LORD is from eternity to

33

eternity toward those who fear him, and his justice toward children's children among those who keep his covenant and remember to fulfill his precepts" (vv.17,18).

In the Book of Exodus we read such phrases as "In your mercy you led the people you redeemed" (15:13); God will show "mercy down to the thousandth generation" (20:6), and "I who grant mercy to whom I will" (33:19). The theme "his mercy endures forever" runs through the earliest literature and is repeated as a refrain in Psalm 136.

The prophet Nehemiah has the refrain of endless mercy in verse after verse such as 9:17-19; 27-28, and 13:22. In Judith (13:14) and Esther (B:6) the theme is that God punished the people for their sins by withholding His mercy. Isaiah uses this theme in the earlier parts, and counters in the latter parts by prophesying that God will return to showing mercy to a repentant people.

Daniel, in passages such as 3:89, gives as a proof of God's goodness that "His mercy endures forever." The last books of the Old Testament still urge that theme of asking for mercy to become worthy of receiving it (see Rom. 1:9).

A thought to be added: the Hebrew term for 'mercy' actually embraces a wider concept than the English word. "Loving mercy" or "merciful love" is a closer equivalent.

Also the word "fear" in scriptural usage, unless the context shows a narrow usage only, covers a much wider concept. Many times the word "serve" is just as meaningful. Thus: "His mercy lasts from age to age for those who 'serve' Him" is probably closer to the true meaning of the text.

3. Patristic use

The title "Our Lady of Mercy" came into use in patristic times, and the concept of reaching to mercy of God through Our Lady's intercession is well known. The famous passage of St. Bernard's used in the prologue is probably the most eloquent. This history of the Order of Our Lady of Mercy, the Mercedarians, founded at the beginning of the thirteenth century by St. Peter Nolasco, was a testimony to Christian mercy in working to free slaves.

St. Augustine sums up this notion of mercy at work in *The City of God*, Bk. 10, No. 6: "Works of mercy done either to ourselves or to our neighbor and referred to God are true sacrifices. Works of mercy are performed for no other reason than to free us from wretchedness and by this means to make us happy.

It clearly follows that the whole redeemed city, that is the assembly and fellowship of the saints, is offered to God as a universal sacrifice through the great High Priest, who, in the nature of a slave, offered Himself for us in His passion in order that we might be the body of so great a Head."

St. Peter Damian: On the Nativity of the Blessed Virgin Mary

"He who is mighty has done great things for you and has given you all power in heaven and on earth. Nothing is impossible to you. You can even give hope to the desperate!

"How can Power itself refuse you power when He took His flesh from you. You can approach that golden altar of human reconciliation, not simply to ask, but even to command — no longer a handmaid, but the Queen.

"Your very nature and power move you to act on your behalf, since the more powerful you are, the more merciful you will be. Power is more glorious when it is exercised in forgiveness.

"Turn back to us in love. I know, O Lady, that you are most loving, that you love us with an invincible love. In you and through you, your Son and God has loved us with the highest love. Who knows how often you have held back God's anger, when justice was about to go forth from the throne of God?

"Turn back to us in your understanding love. In your hands are all the treasures of divine mercy, and you alone have been chosen to dispense such graces. May your hand never fail when you seek occasion to save the weak or pour out your mercy. Your glory is not diminished, but increased, when sinners receive mercy and the just are taken up in glory."

In his touching Homily on the Seven Words, St. Robert Bellarmine links the quality of mercy in God with the maternal qualities of Mary.

"The task that Our Lord gave to St. John of caring for the Virgin Mother was certainly a light burden and a sweet yoke. Who would not joyfully take into his own home the Mother in whose womb the Word lived for nine months and under whose loving care He lived for thirty years?

"Who would not envy this beloved disciple of the Lord, who, when his Lord was gone, was granted the presence of the Mother? And yet I feel that I can say that we, too, may have her presence granted by our prayers. The most merciful Lord, Who was born for us and, in His great love for us, was crucified for us, will respond to say to each of us, 'Behold your Mother'; and to her, 'Behold, each one of these, your sons and daughters.'

"This most loving Master is not sparing of His graces to those who approach His throne with faith and confidence, with a contrite and humble heart, with sincerity. Since He wishes to make us co-heirs to His entire kingdom, certainly He will not hesitate to make us co-heirs to the love of His Mother.

"Nor will this most loving Virgin hesitate to embrace in her maternal love so great a multitude of children. She ardently desires that not a single soul perish whom her Son has redeemed by His precious Blood in His saving death.

"Let us draw near to the throne of Christ's grace with confidence. Let us humbly beg, even with tears, that He will turn to His Mother and say, 'Behold, these are your children'; and to each and every one of us, 'Behold, your Mother and Mine!' "

Modern commentators

In the English-speaking world we are all very familiar with the many and various congregations of religious sisters using the title "Sisters of Mercy." There are innumerable hospitals, schools, and churches using the title "Our Lady of Mercy."

Abbot Columba Marmion, O.S.B., traces the divine mercy as it is imaged in every mother's soul, and pre-eminently in the Blessed Mother, in his book *Christ in His Mysteries.*

"She saw in this child, a child like other children, the very Son of God. Mary's soul was full of immense faith which went far beyond the faith of all the just of the Old Testament; therefore in her Son she saw her God.

"This faith translated itself outwardly in an act of adoration. As soon as she looked upon Jesus, the Maiden-Mother adored Him with an intensity we cannot conceive.

"To this intense faith, this deep adoration, were added the transports of an incommensurable love, a love both human and supernatural.

"God is love, and so that we may have some idea of this love, He gives a share of it to mothers. The heart of a mother, with her unwearying tenderness, the constancy of her solicitude, the inexhaustible delicacy of her affection, is a truly divine creation, although God has placed in her only a spark of His love for us. Yet, however imperfectly a mother's heart reflects the divine love toward us, God gives us our mothers to take His place in some manner with us. He places them at our side, from our cradle, to guide us, guard us, especially in our earliest years when we have so much need of tenderness.

"Hence imagine with what divine predilection the Holy Trinity fashioned the heart of the Blessed Virgin chosen to be the Mother of the Incarnate Word. God delighted in pouring forth love in her heart, in forming it expressly to love the God-Man.

"In Mary's heart were perfectly harmonized the adoration of a creature toward her God, and the love of a mother for her only Son.

"The supernatural love of Our Lady is not less wonderful. As you know, a soul's love for God is measured by its degree of grace. . . . But Our Lady's soul is of perfect purity; unstained by sin, untouched by any shadow of a fault, she is full of grace. . . .

"Jesus gave Himself to Mary in such an ineffable manner, and Mary corresponded so fully, that after the union of the Divine Persons in the Trinity, and the hypostatic union of the Incarnation, we cannot conceive one greater nor deeper.

"Let us draw near to Mary with a humble but entire confidence. If her Son is the Savior of the world, she enters too deeply into His mission not to share the love that He bears to sinners. 'O Mother of our Redeemer,' let us sing to her with the Church, *Alma Redemptoris Mater.* . . . 'You bore your Creator while yet remaining a virgin, succor this fallen race which your Son came to save in taking from us a human nature. Have pity on the sinners whom your Son came to redeem.' For, O Mary, it was to redeem us that He descended from the eternal splendors into your virginal bosom."

Carroll Stuhlmueller, C.P.: The Gospel According to Luke
Vv. 48-50: "The first stanza extols the fruits of faith and of lowly dependence on the merciful God. Luke has already cast Mary in the role of handmaid before God (1:38). So evident will be the transition God has achieved in Mary,

of loneliness turned into fruitfulness, that all men will find hope. There is, therefore, a prophetic or eschatological ring to Mary's words, strengthened by the Old Testament allusions. God appears as the Mighty One; yet He exercises his power most of all in caring for the needy."

5. Meditation

To be a "god-fearing man" has a ring of righteousness and spiritual nobility about it. We think of phrases like "to serve the Lord in fear and trembling." Indeed, when we think of the majesty and power of God, when we consider Him the Creator and ourselves the creature, the sinner, religion does have a shade of fear to it. "The fear of the Lord is the beginning of wisdom."

But for the Christian, "perfect love casts out fear." That is our goal and our vocation. Seeking to serve the Lord, we become joyfully conscious of the mercy of God at work in us and around us and through us. The only fear that lovers have is the fear that they will not please the beloved. Conscious of the mercy of God available to us, we have great confidence in the name we bear as Christians.

Luke 1:51

1. Text

"He has shown might with his arm; he has confused the proud in their inmost thoughts." (NAB)

"He has used the power of his arm, he has routed the arrogant of heart." (NJB)

"He has done valiantly with the strength of his arm, driv-

ing the proud astray in the conceit of their hearts.
(Knox)

"He hath shown strength with his arm; he hath scattered
the haughty in the conceit of their hearts." (Spencer)

"His arm achieves the mastery: he routs the haughty and
proud of heart." (Kleist)

"He has shown might with his arm, he has scattered the
proud in the conceit of their heart." (CCD)

2. Old Testament themes

Again we have a familiar Old Testament theme, the
might of God versus the pride of man. Man may do his best
to frustrate the plans of God, but the power of God is invincible and His will will triumph.

In Job, we see this theme clearly. "He frustrates the
plans of the cunning, so that their hands achieve no suc-
cess; He catches the wise in their own ruses, and the designs of the crafty are routed" (5:12-13).

And if we turn to the Book of Psalms, there are many
examples of God's unsurpassable might. "God is terrible in
the council of the holy ones; he is great and awesome
beyond all around about him. O LORD, God of hosts, who is
like you? Mighty are you, O LORD, and your faithfulness
surrounds you . . . with your strong arm you have scattered
your enemies" (Ps. 89:8-11).

And again: "The LORD is exalted, yet the lowly he sees,
and the proud he knows from afar" (Ps. 138:6).

The idea of God frustrating the proud and haughty in
favor of the meek and the righteous is also a favorite in the
historical books and in the prophetic literature. Esther
prays that the proud Haman may not effect the destruction
of the Jews in her land. In Maccabees the whole thrust of
the book is the struggle between the God-fearing Jews and
the proud oppressors around them.

In fact, going right back to the Pentateuch, we have such stories as Joseph being oppressed in Egypt until his faithfulness moves God to raise him to a position we would probably consider that of "Prime Minister." The struggle of Moses and Aaron versus a Pharoah whose heart had been hardened leads to the triumph of the Exodus events.

St. Peter shows this same awareness when he counsels his readers, in the words of Proverbs 3:34, "In your relations with one another, clothe yourselves with humility, because 'God is stern with the arrogant, but to the humble he shows kindness.' Bow humbly under God's mighty hand, so that in due time he may lift you high" (1 Peter 5:5-6).

The arrogance of the Roman rulers rankled on all the Jews in Christ's time. Both Mary and St. Peter show their awareness of this. They confidently expected God to intervene in His own good time. That it was to be done through a spiritual kingdom far superior to the Roman Empire was a lesson the Apostles had to learn a bit more slowly. It can be disputed whether Mary knew this from the beginning or not, but I suspect she did, though not in any special detail.

3. Patristic use

That God would confuse the proud, that He would use His power to save the humble, was a theme that led St. Bernard to consider the humility that Christ exercised in the Incarnation. See how he develops that theme in this excerpt from the First Homily on the *Missus Est*:

"And He was subject to them. Who? And to whom? God was subject to man! God, I repeat, to whom the angels are subject, whom Principalities and Powers obey, was subject to Mary, and not only to Mary, but to Joseph, too, because of Mary.

"Wonder, indeed, at both, but choose which is the more wonderful. Is it that most loving condescension of the Son,

41

or the tremendous dignity of the Mother? Both are astonishing; both miraculous.

"God submitting in obedience to a woman is indeed humility without equal; the woman commanding her God is sublime beyond measure. In praising virgins we read that they follow the Lamb wherever He goes. How can we praise enough the Virgin who leads Him?

"Learn, O man, to obey. Learn, O earth, to be subject. Learn, O dust, to bow down. In speaking of our Creator, the Evangelist says, 'And He was subject to them,' that is, to Mary and Joseph.

"Blush, O proud ashes! God humilitates Himself and you exalt yourselves. God subjected Himself to man, but you, desiring to dominate your fellowman, place yourselves above your Creator. If it should ever happen that I would want to lord it over others, then may God lovingly rebuke me as He did the Apostle when He said, 'Get behind me, Satan,' for you do not delight in the things of God. . . .

"If you cannot follow Him wherever He goes, then at least deign to follow Him when He humbles Himself for you. If you cannot follow the sublime pathways of virginity, at least follow the safest of pathways, humility. . . .

"The sinful man who chooses to follow in humility has a much safer path than the proud man who tries to follow in virginity. Humble reparation cleanses the former, even as pride spoils the cleanness of the other."

The Fathers saw the mighty power of God at work not only because He was the "Lord God of Hosts," the powerful supporter of Israel's armies, but in His power over nature and His power in the realm of grace. They loved to juxtapose the two sides, as St. Augustine did in his Treatise on the Creed for Catechumens:

"Death came through a woman;
    "Life came through a woman.
 "Eve brought ruin;

"Mary brought salvation.

"Eve was misled by the devil;

"Mary, the Virgin, gave birth to the Savior.

"Eve freely gave in to the temptation of the serpent, shared it with her man, and both merited death.

"Mary, infused with heavenly grace, brought forth the life by which mortal flesh is restored to life.

"Who is the author of this? The Son of the Virgin and the Spouse of virgins, who caused the fruitfulness of His Mother without taking anything away from her virginity."

4. Modern usage

Father John P. Kealy, S.C. Sp.: Luke's Gospel Today

"Through a series of antitheses, the proud and the mighty and the lowly, the hungry and the rich, Luke describes the mighty deeds of reversal, by Yahweh, or the situation of the world. It should be remembered that for Luke the *gift* of the Father, *the* example of 'good things' is the Holy Spirit.

"For Luke, the truly great people are the least. He is well aware of the corrupt pseudo-great in his society, those motivated by self-interest, the greedy politicians. He stresses the necessity of suffering, which is basic to true glory."

Father Raymond E. Brown: The Birth of the Messiah

"The poverty and hunger of the oppressed in the Magnificat are primarily spiritual, but we should not forget the physical realities faced by early Christians. The first followers of Jesus were Galileans; and Galilee, victimized by the absentee ownership of estates, was the spawning ground of first-century revolts against a repressive occupation and the taxation it engendered.

"There was real poverty among the Jerusalem Christians, who became the nucleus of the post-Resurrection

Church. And when the gospel was proclaimed in the Diaspora among Jews and Gentiles, frequently it attracted the underprivileged social classes. . . .

"And so vv. 51-53 of the Magnificat would resonate among such groups; for them the Christian good news meant that the ultimately blessed were not the mighty and the rich who tyrannized them. Reformers of all times have advocated revolutions that would level class distinctions by making the poor sufficiently rich and the powerless sufficiently powerful.

"But the Magnificat anticipates the Lucan Jesus in preaching that wealth and power are not real values since they have no standing in God's sight. This is not an easy message even for those who profess credence in Jesus.

"By introducing it as a leitmotiv in the hymns of the infancy narrative, Luke has begun to introduce the offense of the cross into the good news proclaimed by Gabriel. If for Luke Mary is the first Christian disciple, it is fitting that he place on her lips sentiments that Jesus will make the hallmark of the disciple in the main gospel story.

"It is no accident, then, that some of the offense of the cross rubbed off on Mary. In the early dialogue between Christians and Jews one of the objections against Christianity is that God would never have had His Messiah come into the world without fitting honor and glory, born of a woman who admitted that she was no more than a handmaid, a female slave."

5. Meditation

The mighty of this world tell us that it is better to be rich and powerful and that that is certainly a mark of God's special love for them. Mary tells us that quite the opposite may be true. Might and wealth and power are as fleeting as youth and beauty. In the end, death takes all earthly splendor away.

What remain are virtues and the good works that make our faith and hope come alive. These alone can we take with us to the judgment seat of God. The proud man must show wisdom by bowing before the might of God. Because God is mighty, He can do great works even in such creatures as mankind.

Luke 1:52

1. Text

"He has deposed the mighty from their thrones and raised the lowly to high places." (NAB)

"He has pulled down princes from their thrones and raised high the lowly." (NJB)

"He has put down the mighty from their seat, and exalted the lowly." (Knox)

"He hath cast down potentates from thrones, while exalting the lowly." (Spencer)

"He puts down princes from their thrones, and exalts the lowly." (Kleist)

"He has put down the mighty from their thrones, and has exalted the lowly." (CCD)

2. Old Testament roots

As throughout the Magnificat, there are direct allusions to the Son of Hannah in 1 Sam. 2. "The LORD makes poor and makes rich, he humbles, he also exalts" (v. 7). As every commentator has noted, the canticle of Hannah and the canticle of Mary are woven from the same cloth, the same tradition.

For some reason that I do not fully grasp, almost all the patristic references to the Book of Job call the main protagonist "Holy Job." There are certainly echoes of Holy Job in this prayer. "He sets up on high the lowly, and those who mourn he exalts to safety" (Jb. 5:11). And also, "He loosens the bonds imposed by kings, and leaves but a waistcloth to bind the king's own loins" (12:18).

We can also find traces in the various psalms, such as "But God is the judge; one he brings low; another he lifts up" (Ps. 75:8) and "The LORD sustains the lowly; the wicked he casts to the ground" (Ps. 147:6).

3. Patristic usage

The theme of the low estate of Mary and the high dignity to which she was called resounds through many patristic writings about Mary.

St. Ambrose: Second Book on Luke

"The divine mysteries are indeed hidden, nor are they easy for anyone (according to the prophetic word) who tries to penetrate the counsel of God. However, from certain facts, and from the deeds of Our Lord and Savior, we are able to know and to come a little closer to that divine plan which chose directly that she who was to bear the Lord would be espoused to a man.

"Why was that plan not begun before she was espoused? Perhaps so that it could not be said that she had conceived in adultery.

"And the angel came to her in whom we discern virginity in manner, modesty, word, and virtue. We expect a true virgin to be modest, to avoid friendship with men, and to be careful of conversation with them. Let all young women learn to profit by this example of modesty.

"Only an angel might approach this chamber which was open to no man's view. There alone, without compan-

46

ions or witnesses, with no one to distract her by vain conversation, there she was saluted by the angel.

"Only an angel, no mere man, could bring a message so full of mysterious import. For the first time these words are heard, "The Holy Spirit shall come upon you.' They are heard and believed. And then her reply, 'Behold the handmaiden of the Lord. Be it done to me according to your word.'

"See the humility. Note well the devotion. She who had been chosen to be the Mother of the Lord calls herself His little servant-girl. She certainly does not become haughty over His promise of so exalted a position. By calling herself a handmaiden she does not take as a right what is so freely given as a grace."

St. John Damascene: Second Sermon of the "Falling Asleep" of the Blessed Virgin Mary

"Today the sacred and living Ark of the living God, in whose womb was conceived the Creator, rests in the temple of the Lord, a temple not built by hands. David, her father, leaps for joy, and even the angels join him in exultation.

"On this feast day the archangels celebrate, the Virtues glorify God, the Principalities exult and are joined in praise by the Powers. The Dominations rejoice and the Thrones cannot restrain their happiness. Cherubim and Seraphim proclaim her glory.

"Today the Eden of the new Adam receives that living Paradise in which the condemnation of old was dissolved, in which was planted the Tree of Life, through which our nakedness was covered.

"Today the Immaculate Virgin, in whom there is no spot of earthly taint, but only the love of heavenly delights, today she returns, not to dust but she is brought into the mansions of heaven — she, herself, a living heaven! From her the source of all life was given to mankind. How then could she ever taste death?

"She yielded to that law decreed by Him whom she had borne. As a daughter of Adam she submitted to that ancient law, for her Son, who is Life itself, had not refused it. However, as the Mother of the Living God she was rightfully brought up to Him.

"Eve, who had assented to the seduction of the serpent, was condemned to the pains of childbirth and the sentence of death, as well as being detained below. But this blessed woman had listened to the Word of God, had been filled with the Holy Spirit, had agreed to the message of the archangel, and had brought forth the Son of God without sensual pleasure or male seed.

"She was totally consecrated to God. How could she possibly feel the pains of childbirth, or know death and corruption, or be detained below? In her body she carried life. How definite, how direct, how certain her way to heaven!

" 'Where I am,' says the Life and the Truth which is Christ, 'there shall my servant be.' How much more so, then, that His Mother should be joined to Him.

"From slave-girl to Queen of Heaven, the saints praised God for this triumph of His power."

4. Modern usage

The power of this lowly girl from Nazareth has been felt by many writers. In their own way they acknowledged that God has raised her to high places. I was very moved by the story of Gilbert Keith Chesterton's account of what finally prompted him to become a Catholic. His biographer Michael Ffinch records the moment. It happened in Brindisi, Italy, at Mass on Easter Sunday, 1920.

"Now I can scarcely remember a time when the image of Our Lady did not stand up in my mind quite definitely, at the mention or the thought of all these things. I was quite distant from these things, and then doubtful about these things; and then disputing with the world for them, and with myself against them; for that is the condition before conversion.

"But whether the figure was distant, or was dark and mysterious, or was a scandal to my contemporaries, or was a challenge to myself — I never doubted that this figure was the figure of the Faith; that she embodied, as a complete human being still only human, all that this Thing had to say to humanity.

"The instant I remembered the Catholic Church, I remembered her; when I tried to forget the Catholic Church, I tried to forget her; when I finally saw what was nobler than my fate, the freest and the hardest of all my acts of freedom, it was in front of a gilded and very gaudy little image of her in the port of Brindisi that I promised the thing that I would do, if I returned to my own land" (*G.K. Chesterton* by Michael Ffinch).

Bishop Charles Francis Buddy, the first bishop of San Diego, California, was very energetic in the field of convert-making. Near the end of his career, his friends prevailed upon him to publish some of his apologetic material and his sermons. In the volume *Going Therefore, Teach . . .* he has this to say about the Immaculate Conception:

"The Gospel of St. Luke describes what happened when almighty God sent the angel Gabriel to Nazareth to announce to the Virgin Mary that she had been chosen to be the Mother of God. Our Blessed Mother clarifies an important truth; namely that while charity has first place in the spiritual order, God grants His grace only to the humble.

"It may help our grasp of this essential, to reflect on the satisfying definition of Dom Belorgey, who writes, 'Humility is the truth about our relations with God, recognized by our intelligence, accepted by our will, and realized in our whole life' (*L'humilité benedictine*).

"Too often we underrate the virtue of humility as a mere ornament. Some fail to understand that, to be humble, one need not deny gifts of mind and spirit that God has given. In reality, humility is a fundamental based on the truth of what our divine Benefactor has vouchsafed to us. The Blessed Virgin Mary, who excelled in humility, openly acknowledged that God 'has done great things' for her.

"From the dawn of Christianity, in view of the words spoken by the angel at her Annunciation, Catholics have believed that the Blessed Mother of God was conceived without the stain of original sin. This sublime privilege came to her through the merits of her divine Son, Jesus Christ.

"This doctrine was not defined until December 8, 1854, when Pope Pius IX made it an article of faith. But long before, in 1477, Pope Sixtus IV built and dedicated the Sistine Chapel in honor of the Immaculate Conception. When Pope Pius IX defined the dogma, he did not promulgate a new truth. It always was believed. He simply removed it from the realm of controversy."

5. Meditation

The might of kings and emperors is the stuff of romantic fiction. Whether Caesar or Napoleon, they cannot outlast death or any other event decreed by God. Napoleon even declared that he could destroy the Church, but the Church lives on and Napoleon died in prison.

Stalin sneered, "How many legions has the Pope?" but Stalin and the dictators of his day are long since dead, and the papacy continues. Power is exercised only at the tolerance of God, and "those who are mighty" all have to render an account of their stewardship.

Mary understood how transitory is the power and the

glory of this world. At any time, God can take even the lowliest of people and raise them up to the offices and duties He wills for them.

In the eyes of the world, Mary was the lowliest of the lowly. She was a woman in a world that considered them second-class citizens, if citizens at all. She lived in the poverty of a small village in the hill country of a conquered province on the far edge of the Empire. Could anything good come out of Nazareth?

Only by the power of God could her lowliness be exalted, and it was, indeed.

Luke 1:53

1. Text

"The hungry he has given every good thing, while the rich he has sent empty away." (NAB)

"He has filled the starving with good things, sent the rich away empty." (NJB)

"He has filled the hungry with good things, and sent the rich away empty-handed." (Knox)

"He hath filled the hungry with good things, while sending the rich away empty." (Spencer)

"He fills the hungry with blessings, and sends away the rich with empty hands." (Kleist)

"He has filled the hungry with good things, and the rich he has sent away empty." (CCD)

2. Old Testament themes

Whenever a movie producer wanted to show the decadence of the late Roman Empire, there was a mandatory banquet scene, or even an orgy scene. The movies with biblical themes always had the banquet, whether it was Herod condemning St. John the Baptizer, Daniel reading the handwriting on the wall, or Queen Jezebel plotting her worst against the prophets.

The truth is that the ordinary people did not eat well. Their food was bland and seldom varied. They lived close to the land and the flocks, which provided their meals, substantial under good circumstances but with little variety. There would have been fruit in season, some fish, and a bitter wine.

Originally nomadic, the patriarchs followed the flocks in search of water and grass. In bad times they suffered. In fact, at the head of the biblical story we have Jacob sending to Egypt for food in time of famine, and Joseph recognizing his brothers.

In the story of the Exodus, the people murmured against Moses and Aaron when water became scarce and when there was a lack of meat. This constant attention to such a basic need as nourishment was a natural part of Mary's prayer of joy.

The literal meaning of this verse, that God would give food to the poor while rejecting the arrogant rich, is quite Old Testament. The point — that Mary may well have been marveling that the spiritual food of welcoming the Messiah and receiving of His fullness had been given to the poor class with which she identified and not going to the establishment — is well worth pondering.

This spiritual meaning is justified, since the key to obtaining the favor of plentiful food was the righteousness of the petitioner.

As for the wording, we must consider Psalm 34:11. "The great grow poor and hungry; but those who seek the LORD want for no good thing" and Psalm 107:9 "Because he satisfied the longing soul and filled the hungry soul with good things."

In Hannah's prayer we read: "The well-fed hire themselves out for bread, while the hungry batten on spoil" (1 Sam. 2:5).

3. Patristic usage

St. Ambrose: Homily on Luke

"It is clear to everyone that when faith is demanded, the reason for believing must be shown. Therefore, when the angel announced so mysterious a message to Mary, he immediately gave as proof the news that the elderly, sterile Elizabeth had conceived, 'that you may realize all things are possible with God.'

"When Mary heard this she hastened off to the mountain village, not because she was incredulous about the prophecy, uncertain about the messenger, or doubtful about the fact. She went to rejoice in the answer to prayer; she was prepared to help in fraternal charity; she hastened to participate in happiness.

"When one is filled with God, it is natural to desire to advance still further. Indeed, the Holy Spirit expects us to make good use of grace.

"We can learn to advance in virtue from the example of Mary. See her solicitude for a relative who was with child. Mary's modesty, which previously kept her from much contact with people, did not keep her from undertaking a difficult journey when a work of charity was involved.

When the Virgin knew she was needed, she did not think up excuses or plead the weakness of her sex. She left home immediately and hastened into the mountain country to be of service. Young women, follow this example. Do not waste time in idle visits or public gossip.

"Mary left home promptly when needed, and even remained three months in her cousin's service. Learn modesty from Mary and learn humility. She visits simply as a cousin from some distance, as a junior to a senior. Not only did this noble Virgin come, she was the first to offer a greeting.

"Mary knew that virginity and humility go hand in hand. She was willing to defer to others. She is the teacher of humility who is the perfect example of purity. Humility is essential to faith and truth.

"Meditate on this. The superior comes to the lesser one: Mary to Elizabeth, Christ to John. Afterwards, too, Christ comes to John to sanctify John's baptismal rite in the River Jordan.

"Notice how quickly benefits result from Mary's visit and Christ's presence. Elizabeth first heard Mary's voice, but John first sensed the nearness of grace. Elizabeth heard in the natural order; John exulted in the mysterious order of grace. Elizabeth acknowledges Mary; John responds to Christ.

"The two mothers speak words of grace; the two infants communicate on the spiritual plane. As the mothers draw close in fraternal charity, by a twofold miracle, they prophesy in the spirit of their children.

"The baby exults and the mother is filled with the Holy Spirit. When the son receives the Holy Spirit first, only then does his mother receive it — it is through him. Then she cried out 'How wonderful it is that that mother of my Lord comes to me!' That is: this is a great and unexpected honor that the Mother of the Lord, a woman so singularly chosen, should be coming here to see me. I sense the miracle. I acknowledge the mystery — the Mother of my Lord even now carries the Divine Word within her."

St. John Chrysostom: Metaphrasten
"The Son of God did not choose for his Mother some rich or wealthy noble, but rather that Blessed Virgin whose

54

soul was so rich in virtue. This blessed woman, Mary, conceived Christ in her womb because she preserved her chastity above all of human nature. . . .

"She, alone, excels in heaven and earth. Who is holier than she? Not prophets, not martyrs, not patriarchs. No, not angels, Thrones, Dominations, Seraphim, nor Cherubim. No creature visible or invisible can be found to excel her. She is the handmaiden and the Mother of God."

4. Recent usage

Rev. G. Graystone, S.M.: "The Mother of Jesus in the Scripture."

"Stimulated by the realization that Elizabeth, through divine light, knows what has taken place, Mary breaks her silence, and emotions long pent-up find expression in a spontaneous outburst of praise and gratitude to Him who has done great things for her. Her thoughts find natural expression in the words of the Old Testament Scriptures.

"It is not of course necessary to suppose that Mary uttered the canticle in precisely the same form in which it has come down to us, or that it perfectly fits its present context, but it well reflects Mary's humility, self-effacement, and habit of tranquil reflection.

"Moreover, as 'Daughter of Sion [Zion]' she voices the sentiments of the people of God. The supernatural conception of Jesus is the apogee of the joyful and miraculous births of the O.T.; hence the Magnificat borrows from the Canticle of Hannah (1 Sam. 2:1-10).

"Still more, as the humble Virgin, does she personify the 'Poor of Yahweh,' whose 'lowliness the Lord has regarded,' echoing the phrases of the Psalms, Prophets, Wisdom Books and Pentateuch. In the name of Abraham's race, she gives thanks that the promises are fulfilled, that the Messiah is here.

"Thus the Magnificat is the model of the prayer of the people of God, the Church; and as the personification of God's messianic people (cf. Mal. 3:12), like the spouse of the Canticles (6:9), Mary exclaims, 'Behold from henceforth all generations shall call me blessed' — because she is the Mother of the Savior. Here devotions to Mary, the archetype of the Church, is foreshadowed."

5. Meditation

The modern, ordinary American citizen, both of the United States and Canada, is rich by comparison with the vast majority of people in the Third World. Poverty exists in the United States, a land blessed with so much material prosperity, but in general we are wealthy by most standards.

Does this cause a twinge of spiritual pain? Will we be among the rich who are sent away with empty hands? Will the poor seize the Kingdom of God and bear it away in triumph, away from us?

There is much here for us to ponder. If our attachment to material goods is too strong, if we are lacking in poverty of spirit, then we should do more than meditate. It is time for a conversion, back to Gospel principles and a return to the charity which brings faith alive.

When we use our material goods and our human talents to help others, then we can hope to share in the Kingdom of God as responsible, productive citizens.

We can also examine our "spiritual hunger." We can work to number ourselves among those "who hunger and thirst after justice" and use the things of this world for spiritual enrichment.

Luke 1:54

1. Text

"He has upheld Israel his servant, ever mindful of his mercy." (NAB)

"He has come to the help of Israel his servant, mindful of his faithful love." (NJB)

"He has protected his servant Israel, keeping his merciful design in remembrance." (Knox)

"He hath succored Israel, his servant, being mindful of his mercy." (Spencer)

"He has given help to Israel his servant, mindful of his mercy." (CCD)

2. Old Testament themes

Mary's spirituality was certainly built on the covenant that God had entered into with Israel: "I will be your God and you will be my people" (Ex. 6:7). There had been a covenant between God and Abraham and a further refinement of this with God and Moses on behalf of the people. Because of this special treaty, Israel could call upon its terms for a special, a "faithful mercy." This is what Mary is referring to in this verse.

It is reminiscent of Isaiah 41:8-10. "But you, Israel, my servant, Jacob, whom I have chosen, offspring of Abraham my friend — You whom I have taken from the ends of the earth and summoned from its far-off places, You whom I have called my servant, whom I have chosen and will not cast off — Fear not, I am with you; be not dismayed; I am your God. I will strengthen you and uphold you with my right hand of justice."

There is also the echo of several Psalm themes, especially Ps. 98:3 "He has remembered his kindness and his faithfulness toward the house of Israel. All the ends of the earth have seen the salvation by our God." In Psalm 136 the entire song has, as the conclusion for each verse, "for his mercy endures forever."

The theme of Maccabees is that God will show mercy and be faithful to his promises if the people turn back to God in sincerity. In the midst of bitter persecution the people invoke the covenant and seek for God's merciful help.

3. Patristic usage

The saints loved to salute Mary, the Mother of the Lord, as a true Jew, the Daughter of Zion, the descendant from the patriarchs, starting with Abraham. God's promise of an everlasting king of the line of David depended for its fulfillment on Mary's lineage, literally, and Joseph's descent legally.

St. Bernard: On the Aquaduct

"From such seed as this, the priestly rod produced fruit in great measure. Drawing from these sublime fountains, Mary has poured forth upon us the nourishing drink of great profit. She who is on a heavenly plane beyond all the angels had received the Word from the heart of the Father Himself.

"For this is the new day of creation, the day on which the Father gives the light of salvation. But is it not also the Virgin's day, when she approaches bright and shining as the dawn, beautiful as the moon, radiant as the sun! (Canticle 6:10).

"Truth has finally returned to the earth, not through angelic creatures nor through any individual angel but through this daughter of Abraham. Great as the angels are whom minister to God, Mary far surpasses them, for she has been chosen not as servant, but as Mother."

St. Thomas Aquinas: Summa Contra Gentiles: 4:34

"A man is properly called the son of his mother because he receives his body from her. He does not receive his soul from her, but from something exterior. The body of this Man has been taken from the Virgin Mother.

"Obviously, the body of this Man is the body of the natural Son of God, that is, the Word of God. Therefore it is absolutely correct to call the Blessed virgin The Mother of the Word of God,' and "The Mother of God,' even though the Godhead, or divinity, was not taken from her. The designation 'son' does not mean that a man has taken his entire being from his mother, but only his body.

"St. John says "The Word was made flesh." He would not have flesh unless He took it from the woman, namely the Virgin Mary. Therefore we can repeat, the Virgin is the Mother of the Word of God.

"St. Paul says in the Epistle to the Romans, 'Christ, who is above all things God, blessed forever more, is a descendant of the Patriarchs according to the flesh.' He would not have this carnal descent except for the Virgin. Therefore, He who is God, who is above all created things, has His body from the Virgin. We can rightly call the Virgin the Mother of God Incarnate."

4. Modern usage

Vatican II: Lumen Gentium, No. 9

"The Israel of old was already called the Church of God while it was on pilgrimage through the desert. So, the New Israel, as it makes its way in this present age, seeking a city that is to come, a city that will remain, is also known as the Church of Christ, for He acquired it by His own Blood, filled it with His Spirit and equipped it with appropriate means to be a visible and social unity.

"God has called together the assembly of those who in

faith look on Jesus, the author of salvation and the principle of unity and peace, and so has established the Church to be for each and for all the visible sacrament of this unity which brings salvation."

Father Charles E. Coughlin: "By the Sweat of Thy Brow"

"Bear with me, my friends, if I appear to be dabbling in superlatives while speaking of the superlative work fashioned by the hand of God. At least we can be historians in calmness. May I recall for you the plight of women in the days of Augustus Caesar at Rome, or in the reign of the majestic Pericles in Athens? Woman was always a chattel, always a thing.

"Not only was she denied the rights of citizenship, but she was bought and traded as a man would purchase or sell a horse. Nevertheless, it was her hand which was supposed to rock the cradle of progress. It was her breast that was supposed to feed the citizen.

"Not until Mary, the immaculate virgin mother, came upon the horizon of history, did the noble soul of womanhood begin to cast its warmth and benediction upon the works and destinies of humankind. Men may boast of their valor and courage; but the Christian woman is praised for her love and her sacrifice. Men may be renowned for their intelligence and inventiveness, but women will always be known for their motherliness — a word which compounds every beautiful quality which enters into the vocabulary of man.

Therefore, Mary stands alone, "our tainted nature's solitary boast" [William Wordsworth], the one spotless creature, unblemished by sin! She is the ideal to which we aspire, the tender mother not only of Christ, but of everyone of Christ's brothers and sisters who are not forgetful either of Bethlehem's miracle or Calvary's tragedy."

5. Meditation

How many times in its history, the Church, the new Israel of God, has been pronounced dead or dying! It survived the catacombs and the Roman emperors. It endured the so-called Dark Ages and civilized the barbarians who sought to conquer. It passed through the "Enlightenment," the "Age of Reason," the French Revolution and the years of Napoleon.

Today the Church suffers behind the Iron Curtain, in Lithuania, Poland, and China. It suffers in the poverty and injustice of its children in the Third World. And yet the Church keeps the Faith.

It takes Mary's prayer very personally, "He has upheld Israel his servant, ever mindful of his mercy." We still pray for the faithfulness and dedication to Christ that will bring to us to share the mercy and strength of the Father.

The ancient adage is true, "The blood of martyrs is the seed of Christians." Or the recurrent theme in Church history, noted by St. John in the Book of Revelation: when the Church appears rich, it is poor; when it seems impoverished, it is spiritually rich (see Rev. 3:5-16).

St. John Chrysostom, in his catecheses, likened the Church of his times to the Israelites in the time of the Exodus.

He writes, "The Israelites witnessed marvels; you will also witness marvels, greater and more splendid than those which accompanied them on their departure from Egypt. You did not see Pharoah drowned with his armies, but you have seen the devil with his weapons overcome by the waters of baptism.

"The Israelites passed through the sea; you have passed from death to life. They were delivered from the Egyptians; you have been delivered from the powers of darkness. The Israelites were freed from slavery to a pagan people; you have been freed from the much greater slavery of sin."

61

Luke 1:55

1. Text

"Even as he promised our fathers, promised Abraham and
his descendants forever." (NAB)

"According to the promise he made to our ancestors — of
his mercy to Abraham and to his descendants forever." (NJB)

"According to the promise which he made to our forefathers, Abraham and his posterity for evermore."
(Knox)

"As he declared to our father, to Abraham and his seed for
ever." (Spencer)

"As he had promised to our fathers — with Abraham and
his posterity forever and evermore." (Kleist)

"Even as he spoke to our fathers — to Abraham and to his
posterity forever." (CCD)

2. Old Testament

By the twelfth chapter, the Book of Genesis gets down
to more serious history with the material on Abraham.
Before that, its theological content overshadows the his-
toricity of the narrative. The frequent use of the story of
Abraham in the New Testament shows how much he
meant to the Jews of this period.

The chapter begins with Abram's call, as he is sent by
the Lord to a land specially chosen by God. The very call
contains the promise, "I will make of you a great nation
and I will bless you; I will make your name great, so that
you will be a blessing. I will bless those who bless you and

curse those who curse you. All the communities of the earth shall find blessing in you" (12:2-3).

When Abraham and his party arrived in Canaan, he was told, "To your descendants I will give this land" (12:7). There, at Bethel, close to Shechem, his point of entrance, Abraham offered the first sacrifice to the Lord. It was in this vicinity that God renewed his promise of the land.

"Look about you, and from where you are, gaze to the north and south, east and west; all the land that you see I will give to you and to your descendants forever. I will make your descendants like the dust of the earth; if anyone could count the dust of the earth, your descendants too might be counted. Set forth and walk about in the land, through its length and breadth, for to you I will give it" (Gn. 13:14-17). It was at this time Abraham built an altar to God at Hebron.

Melchizedek, the mysterious King of Salem, a priest of God most High, also comes along at this point in the story. After this Abraham pleads with God to give him a son, so that the land God has given him can be passed to his descendants. Ishmael is born, the child of Abraham and the slave-girl Hagar, to be followed by the covenant of circumcision, when God again promises the land in perpetuity (see Gn. 17:3-11).

When God put Abraham's faith to the test by seeming to demand the sacrifice of his only legitimate son, Isaac, the child of a wondrous birth from Abraham and Sarah, once more the promise is made to Abraham and his descendant, who will be "as numerous as the stars of the sky and the sands of the seashore," in whom "all the nations of the earth shall find blessing" (see Gn. 22:15-18).

All of this is implied in Mary's use of the name of Abraham. All of the promises made to the Jews in the entire Old Testament are summed up by the use of his name. And now, as Mary exults, those promises are being fulfilled in a way beyond anything that they could have imagined. THE blessing for which all nations would have their ultimate blessing is being given.

Christ, the descendant of Abraham, of the House of David, has come incarnate, through Mary.

Note: the name Abraham occurs over 300 times in the Bible. While we dwell on the fulfillment of the promise in the advent of Christ, you can imagine how in Israel, today, the return of the land itself would be seen as a promise fulfilled.

3. Patristic usage

St. Bernard: First Homily on the Circumcision

"O truly wonderful mystery! The Boy is circumcised and named Jesus. How are these things connected? You would think that circumcision is for those in need of salvation, not for the Savior. You would certainly think it preferable for Him to perform the work of salvation, rather than be the subject of it.

"Yet, see how this Mediator between God and man, from the very instant of His birth, joins the divine and the human, the highest and the lowest. He is born of a woman, but in such a way that the flower of her virginity is not harmed in any way by motherhood.

"He is wrapped in swaddling clothes, but even in this humble garb, He is praised by angelic voices. He is tucked away in a manger, but a radiant star keeps watch.

"The circumcision proves, beyond a shadow of doubt, the fact of His humanity; the Name indicates the majesty of His glory. He was circumcised because He was truly a son of Abraham; He was called Jesus, the Name that is above all names, because He was truly the Son of God."

Novatian: The Trinity

"Therefore, let those who read in the Scripture that the man Christ Jesus is the Son of Man, also read there that this same Jesus is called both God and the Son of God.

"In the same manner that He, as man, is of Abraham, even so, as God, is He also before Abraham himself.

"In the same manner that He, as man, is the Son of David, so He is also, as God, called the Lord of David."

Peter Bloisius: Sermon to Priests, No. 60

"A priest has the primacy of Abel, the patriarchate of Abraham, the government of Noah, the order of Melchizedek, the dignity of Aaron, the authority of Moses, the perfection of Samuel, the power of Peter, the unction of Christ."

4. Modern usage

Abbot Columba Marmion: Christ in His Mysteries —
Divine Preparations

"You know that it was just after the sin of our first parents, in the very cradle of the already rebellious human race, that God began to reveal the mystery of the Incarnation. Adam and Eve, prostrate before the Creator, in the shame and despair of their fall, dare not raise their eyes to heaven. And behold, even before pronouncing the sentence of their banishment from the terrestrial paradise, God speaks to them the first words of forgiveness and hope.

"Instead of being cursed and driven out from the presence of their God, as were the rebel angels, they were to have a Redeemer; He it was who should break the power won over them by the devil. And as their fall began by the prevarication of the woman, it was to be by the son of a woman that this redemption should be wrought. 'I shall place enmity between you and the woman, between her seed and your seed, and He shall crush your head. . . .' (cf. Gn. 3:15).

"This is what is called the 'Proto-Gospel,' the first word of salvation. It is the first promise of redemption, the dawn of divine mercy to the sinful earth, the first ray of light which was one day to vivify the world, the first manifestation of the mystery hidden in God from all eternity.

"After this promise, all the religion of the human race, and later, all the religion of the chosen people is concentrated around the 'seed of the woman' which is to deliver mankind.

"Throughout the years as they pass by, and as the centuries advance, God makes His promise more precise; He repeats it with more solemnity. He assures the patriarchs, Abraham, Isaac, and Jacob, that it is from their race that the blessed seed shall come forth; to the dying Jacob He shows that it is in the tribe of his son Judah that the One Who is to come, the desired of the nations, shall arise."

Father William Maestri: Mary: Model of Justice

"The closing words of the Magnificat remind us of the most important insights of biblical spirituality: God *acts* in human history. The God of Abraham and his descendants does not remain indifferent to the works of His hands. God creates and He cares. God's active word calls all things into being and He is involved in all that unfolds.

"Far from being an absent or spectator God, Yahweh is ever mindful of what takes place on earth. History is more than the passing of events. History is going someplace and it is going to be fulfilled in someone. History is moving toward the Kingdom of God, and when Jesus comes in glory at the *Parousia*, then He will be all in all.

"What we do as individuals, communities and nations makes a difference to God. The words of the Lord's Prayer say it powerfully, 'Thy Kingdom come. Thy will be done on earth as it is in heaven.' "

5. Meditation

That God is faithful to His promises is the theme around which these canticles in Luke are chronicled in this volume. That these promises were fulfilled in history and are being fulfilled in the Church until the end of time is the noble theme of Christian living.

In the Incarnation we see God granting the mercy and the blessing promised to all mankind, to Abraham, and, through him, to us. The Church salutes Abraham as the Father of our faith (Rom 4:18) and so we see not a mere physical fulfillment of promise but a spiritual and eternal fulfillment that goes far beyond the literal.

We see God going beyond the mere words so often: Is. 7:14, "The virgin shall conceive and bear a son and he shall be called 'Emmanuel.' " The name means "God with us," and how exactly that was fulfilled in the Incarnation. God with us, not as a blessing alone but as a presence, a reality, a prophecy fulfilled.

Luke 1:56

MARY REMAINED with Elizabeth about three months and then returned home.

Since Elizabeth was already in her sixth month when Gabriel brought the news to Mary, and since it would take time to arrange to travel to the home of Zachary and Elizabeth — it was a long and difficult journey which a young maiden could not take alone — the three months that Mary spent with Elizabeth would have included the time of the birth and circumcision of St. John the Baptizer.

Mary must have witnessed the events that we will cover next in the verses of the *Benedictus*. Then, as Luke remarks, she returned to her own home, since she had not yet told St. Joseph of her condition. As she was entering the fourth month of her pregnancy, it was a decision that had to be made quite soon.

St. Luke, however, passes over the events of the next few months in Mary's life, and we have to turn to St. Matthew to find out about St. Joseph's ordeal and the angelic (probably St. Gabriel) intervention.

When contemplating Mary's role in the economy of salvation, the liturgy frequently applies to Mary the tribute paid to Judith:

"Blessed are you daughter, by the Most High God, above all the women on earth; and blessed be the Lord God, the creator of heaven and earth, who guided your blow at the head of the chief of our enemies" (Jdt. 13:18).

"You are the glory of Jerusalem, the surpassing joy of Israel. You are the splendid boast of our people (Jdt. 15:9).

Appendix A:
Pope John Paul II

Encyclical 'Mother of the Redeemer'
(Redemptoris Mater),
March 25, 1987

3. The "Magnificat" of the Pilgrim Church

'35. At the present stage of her journey, therefore, the Church seeks to rediscover the unity of all who profess their faith in Christ, in order to show obedience to her Lord, who prayed for this unity before His Passion 'Like a pilgrim on a foreign land, the Church presses forward amid the persecutions of the world and consolations of God, announcing the Cross and Death of the Lord until He comes' (*Lumen Gentium* 8).

'' 'Moving forward through trial and tribulation, the Church is strengthened by the power of God's grace promised to her by the Lord, so that in the weakness of the flesh she may not waver from perfect fidelity, but remain a bride worthy of her Lord; that moved by the Holy Spirit she may never cease to renew herself, until through the Cross she arrives at the light which knows no setting,' (*Lumen Gentium* 9).

''The Virgin Mother is constantly present on this journey of faith of the People of God towards the light. This is shown in a special way by the canticle of the 'Magnificat,' which, having welled up from the depths of Mary's faith at the Visitation, ceaselessly reechoes in the heart of the Church down the centuries. This is proved by its daily recitation in the liturgy of Vespers and at many other moments of both personal and communal devotion.

" 'My soul magnifies the Lord,
and my spirit rejoices in God my Savior,
for he has looked on his servant in her lowliness.
For behold, henceforth all generations shall call
    me blessed;
for he who is mighty has done great things for me,
and holy is his name:
And his mercy is from age to age
on those who fear him.
He has shown strength with his arm,
he has scattered the proud-hearted,
he has cast down the mighty from their thrones,
and lifted up the lowly;
he has filled the hungry with good things,
sent the rich away empty.
He has helped his servant Israel,
remembering his mercy,
as he spoke to our fathers,
to Abraham and to his seed for ever' (Luke
    1:46-55).

"36. When Elizabeth greeted her young kinswoman coming from Nazareth, Mary replied with the 'Magnificat.' In her greeting, Elizabeth first called Mary 'blessed' because of 'the fruit of her womb,' and then she called Mary 'blessed' because of her faith (Lk 1:42, 45). These two blessings referred directly to the Annunciation. Now, at the Visitation, when Elizabeth's greeting bears witness to that culminating moment, Mary's faith acquires a new consciousness and a new expression.

"That which remained hidden in the depths of the 'obedience of faith' at the Annunciation can now be said to spring forth like a clear and life-giving flame of the spirit. The words used by Mary on the threshold of Elizabeth's house are an inspired profession of her faith, in which her response to the revealed word is expressed with the religious and poetical exultation of her whole being toward God.

"In these sublime words, which are simultaneously very simple and wholly inspired by the sacred texts of the people of Israel, Mary's personal experience, the ecstasy of her heart, shines forth. In them shines a ray of the mystery of God, the glory of His ineffable holiness, the eternal love which, as an irrevocable gift, enters into human history.

"Mary is the first to share in this new revelation of God and, within the same, in this new 'self-giving' of God. Therefore she proclaims, 'For He who is mighty has done great things for me, and holy is His name.' Her words reflect a joy of spirit which is difficult to express. 'My spirit rejoices in God my Savior.' Indeed, 'the deepest truth about God and the salvation of man is made clear to us in Christ, who is at the same time the mediator and the fullness of all revelation' (*Dei Verbum* 2).

"In her exultation Mary confesses that she finds herself in the very heart of this fullness of Christ. She is conscious that the promises made to the fathers, first of all 'to Abraham and to his posterity forever,' is being fulfilled in herself. She is thus aware that concentrated within herself as the Mother of Christ is the whole salvific economy, in which 'from age to age' is manifested He who, as the God of the Covenant, 'remembers His mercy.'

"37. The Church, which from the beginning has modeled her earthly journey on that of the Mother of God, constantly repeats after her the words of the *Magnificat*. From the depths of the Virgin's faith at the Annunciation and the Visitation, the Church derives the truth about the God of the Covenant: the God who is Almighty and does 'great things' for man: 'holy is His name.'

"In the *Magnificat* the Church sees uprooted that sin which is found at the outset of the earthly history of man and woman, the sin of disbelief and of 'little faith' in God. In contrast with the 'suspicion' which the 'father of lies' sowed in the heart of Eve the first woman, Mary, whom tradition is wont to call the 'new Eve' (St. Justin, St. Irenaeus, Tertullian, etc.), and the true 'Mother of the living' (St. Epiphanius), boldly proclaims the undimmed truth about God: the holy and almighty God, who from the beginning is the source of all gifts, He who 'has done great things in her' as well as in the whole universe.

"In the act of creation God gives existence to all that is. In creating man, God gives him the dignity of the image and likeness of Himself in a special way as compared with earthly creatures. Moreover, in His desire to give, God gives Himself in the Son, notwithstanding man's sin: He 'so loved the world that he gave His only Son' (Jn. 3:16). Mary is the first witness of this marvelous truth, which will be fully accomplished through 'the works and words' (Acts 1:1) of her Son and definitively through His Cross and Resurrection.

"The Church, which even 'amid trials and tribulations' does not cease repeating with Mary the words of the *Magnificat*, is sustained by the power of God's truth, proclaimed on that occasion with such extraordinary simplicity. At the same time, by means of this truth about God, the Church desires to shed light upon the difficult and sometimes tangled paths of man's earthly existence.

"The Church's journey, therefore, near the end of the second Christian Millennium, involves a renewed commitment to her mission. Following Him who said, '[God] has anointed me to preach good news to the poor' (Lk. 4:18), the Church has sought from generation to generation and still seeks today to accomplish that same mission.

"The Church's love of preference for the poor is wonderfully inscribed in Mary's *Magnificat*. The God of the Covenant, celebrated in the exultation of her spirit by the Virgin of Nazareth, is also He who 'has cast down the mighty from their thrones, and lifted up the lowly . . . filled the hungry with good things, sent the rich away empty . . . scattered the proud-hearted . . . and His mercy is from age to age on those who fear Him.'

"Mary is deeply imbued with the spirit of the 'poor of Yahweh,' who in the prayer of the Psalms awaited from God their salvation, placing all their trust in him (cf. Ps. 25;31;35;55). Mary truly proclaims the coming of the 'Messiah of the poor' (cf. Is. 11:4;61:1). Drawing from Mary's heart, from the depth of her faith expressed in the words of the *Magnificat*, the Church renews ever more effectively in herself the awareness that the truth about God who saves, the truth about God who is the source of every gift, cannot be separated from the manifestation of his love of preference for the poor and humble, that love which, celebrated in the *Magnificat*, is later expressed in the words and works of Jesus.

"The Church is thus aware — and at the present time this awareness is particularly vivid — not only that these two elements of the message contained in the *Magnificat* cannot be separated, but also that there is the duty to safeguard carefully the importance of 'the poor' and of 'the option in favor of the poor' in the world of the living God.

"These are matters and questions intimately connected with the Christian meaning of freedom and liberation. 'Mary is totally dependent upon God and completely directed towards Him, and, at the side of her Son, she is the

73

most perfect image of freedom and of the liberation of humanity and the universe. It is to her as Mother and Model that the Church must look in order to understand in its completeness the meaning of her own mission' (Congregation for the Doctrine of the Faith, 'Christian Freedom and Liberation,' March 22, 1986)."

Section II:
The *Benedictus*

Luke 1:68

''BLESSED BE the Lord, the God of Israel
  because he has visited and ransomed his people.
He has raised a horn of saving strength for us
  in the house of David his servant,
As he promised through the mouths of his holy ones,
  the prophets of ancient times:
Salvation from our enemies
  and from the hands of all our foes.
He has dealt mercifully with our fathers
  and remembered the holy covenant he made,
The oath he swore to Abraham our father he would grant
    us:
  that, rid of fear and delivered from the enemy,
We should serve him devoutly and through all our days
  be holy in his sight.
And you, O child, shall be called
  prophet of the Most High;
For you shall go before the Lord
  to prepare straight paths for him,
Giving his people a knowledge of salvation
  in freedom from their sins,
All this is the work of the kindness of our God;
  he, the Dayspring, shall visit us in his mercy

To shine on those who sit in darkness and in the shadow of
   death,
   to guide our feet into the way of peace.''

Prologue:
Luke 1:63

''[ZECHARIAH] signaled for a writing tablet and wrote the
words, ''John is his name.''

Luke starts off his Gospel narrative with the announcement to the priest Zechariah (or Zachary), ''of the priestly
class of Abijah,'' that his sterile wife, Elizabeth, ''a descendant of Aaron,'' will bear him a son who is to be named
John.

St. Thomas Aquinas is of the opinion that, since the
archangel Gabriel brought the good news to Mary, he
should be considered the ''angel of the Incarnation,'' and
that it is he who is referred to in all the infancy narratives
(cf. *Summa Theologiae*, Bk. 3, Ques. 30).

Zechariah returns home, and in due course, nine
months thereafter, the male child is born. The relatives pre-
sume that he will be named after his father, even though
this was not a customary practice. It is probably further
proof of the advanced age of the parents.

Instead, Elizabeth announces that his name is John. Un-
sure of this, they approach the father and he, gesturing for
a writing tablet, writes, ''His name is John.''

John L. McKenzie, in his *Dictionary of the Bible*, tells
us the meaning of the names in this section of Luke:

''John'' comes from a Hebrew combination which

means "Yahweh is gracious" or, perhaps, "Graced by Yahweh." It denotes a special, loving relationship between God and the person so named.

The name is used for several men in the New Testament, but the men of special interest to us are St. John the Baptizer and St. John the Apostle, "the beloved disciple" and evangelist of the Fourth Gospel.

That it has been very popular among Christians is proved by the fact that the name most often found in the Roman Martyrology is John. The fact that three recent Popes have used the name, and that it is the single most used name in the papacy — all testifies to its popularity. The Cathedral of Rome, and the Mother Church of Christianity, is the Basilica of St. John Lateran, named for the Baptizer.

"Zechariah," or "Zachary," comes from the Hebrew term which means "Yahweh has remembered," or, perhaps, "Remembered by Yahweh." It would be considered a blessing.

It is quite a common name in biblical usage and includes a king of Israel and several prophets. Our special interest lies in the fact that it is the name of the father of St. John the Baptizer, the author of the *Benedictus*.

"Elizabeth" comes from a Hebrew term which means "*El* (God) is fullness," or perhaps, "Filled with God's (graces?)" It, too, is a term of blessing and blessedness, the type of name that would be given to a much loved and longed-for daughter.

It is an ancient name, a name in Jewish antiquity as Miryam (Mary), since it was the name of the wife of the priest Aaron, the brother of Moses.

Elizabeth is the kinswoman, perhaps cousin, of the Blessed Mother, and their visit before the birth of St. John the Baptizer occasioned the *Magnificat*. Luke ends that passage with the announcement of Mary's return home, but she was most probably present for the events of the *Benedictus* passage, Luke simply tidies up one event before going on to the next.

When St. John is named, the sign that Zechariah demanded was fulfilled, and he who had been mute (and maybe deaf?) was released from his bondage and he salutes the power of God with his own canticle, the *Benedictus*.

There is no way of knowing if these are his *exact* words, as was true of the *Magnificat*, but they certainly express his exultation in a way familiar to his Jewish prayer-life. They are the words the Holy Spirit, the co-author of the Holy Scriptures, will have us accept as His feelings and reaction.

Luke 1:68

1. Text

"Blessed be the Lord of God of Israel because he has visited and ransomed his people." (NAB)

"Blessed be the Lord, the God of Israel, for he has visited his people and set them free." (NJB)

"Blessed be the Lord, the God of Israel, he has visited his people and wrought their redemption." (Knox)

"Blessed be the Lord God of Israel, because he hath visited his people and wrought redemption for them." (Spencer)

"Blessed be the Lord, the God of Israel, because he has visited and wrought redemption for his people." (CCD)

2. Old Testament roots

Zechariah's canticle, called the *Benedictus* from the first word in the Latin translation, has been considered a psalm, a prophecy and a typical circumcision prayer. It is all of those things and it is very typical of the Jewish priestly prayer.

Zechariah addresses his prayer by addressing the "Lord God of Israel," a pattern begun at least by Moses who addressed the "God of our fathers" (Ex. 3:15).

The idea of "blessing" God is not the same as we are familiar with, for example, in asking a priest's blessing. The biblical term includes awareness of God's intervention, thanksgiving for it, and, indeed, exultation in that intervention.

David prayed in this way when he saw Solomon installed on the throne, following his father, David, and carrying on the line, as God had promised. "Blessed be the Lord, the God of Israel, who has this day seated one of my sons upon my throne, so that I see it with my own eyes."

The phrase "Blessed be God" is used several times in the Psalter, usually ending the various "books" of Psalms. They include minor variations: "Blessed be the Lord, the God of Israel, from all eternity and forever. Amen. Amen" (Ps. 41:14); "Blessed be the Lord, the God of Israel, who alone does wondrous deeds" (Ps. 72:18), and similar expressions.

The notion of a visitation by God again includes the general idea of a divine intervention. Especially in the New Testament this is usually a favorable, a happy intervention.

Isaiah would speak of God's visitation to avenge Israel on an enemy (see Is. 23:17), but Jeremiah would beg God to visit his people to save them from an enemy to save himself from an enemy (see Jer. 15:15)

So the idea of a visitation, here, is for the purpose of ransoming people enslaved by sins. I think if I were back in

Greek class translating this passage, I might be tempted to translate "ransom" with the word *liberation*.

Ransom is the word used for the sacrifice that had to be offered for each first-born male (see Nm. 18:16). In the Psalms we have this notion applied more widely: "Yet in no way can a man redeem himself or pay his own ransom to God" (Ps. 49:8), and "Come and ransom my life; as an answer for my enemies, redeem me" (Ps. 69:19).

Isaiah cries out, "Is my hand too short to ransom?" (Is. 50:2), and Jeremiah gives as a reason to hope, "The Lord shall ransom Jacob" (Jer. 31:11).

The theme of ransom has New Testament meaning too, with Christ's sacrifice being referred to as the price of our ransom.

3. Patristic themes

Clement of Alexandria: Christ the educator

"This is the greatest and most noble of all God's works: saving mankind. But those who labor under some sickness are dissatisfied if the physician prescribes no remedy to restore their health. How, then, can we withhold our sincerest gratitude from the divine Teacher when He corrects the acts of disobedience that sweep us on to ruin and uproots the desires that drag us into sin, refusing to be silent and connive at them, and even offers counsels on the right way to live? Certainly we owe Him the deepest gratitude.

"That is why the Word is called Savior, because He has left men remedies . . . to effect understanding and salvation, and because, awaiting the favorable opportunity, He corrects evil, diagnoses the causes of passion, extracts the roots of unreasonable lusts, advises what we should avoid, and applies all the remedies of salvation to those who are sick."

"John was born of a woman too old for childbirth; Christ was born of a youthful virgin. The news of John's birth was met with incredulity, and his father was struck dumb. Christ's birth was believed, and he was conceived through faith.

"John appears as the boundary between the two testaments, the old and the new. That he is a sort of boundary the Lord himself bears witness when he speaks of 'the law and the prophets' up until John the Baptizer. Thus he represents times past and is the herald of the new era to come. As a representative of the past, he is born of aged parents; as a herald of the new era, he is declared to be a prophet while still in his mother's womb. . . .

"Zechariah is silent and loses his voice until John, the precursor of the Lord, is born and restores his voice. The silence of Zechariah is nothing but the age of prophecy lying hidden, obscured as it were, and concealed before the preaching of Christ.

"At John's arrival Zechariah's voice is released, and it becomes clear at the coming of the one who was foretold. The release of Zechariah's voice at the birth of John is a parallel to the rending of the veil at Christ's crucifixion.

"If John were announcing his own arrival, Zechariah's lips would not have been opened. The tongue is loosened because a voice is born. For when John was preaching the Lord's coming, he was asked, 'Who are you?' And he replied 'I am the voice of one crying in the wilderness.'

"The voice is John, but the Lord 'in the beginning was the Word.' John was a voice that lasted only for a time; Christ, the Word in the beginning, is eternal."

4. Modern commentators:

Father Carroll Stuhlmueller, C.P.: The Gospel according to Luke

"The first part of the Benedictus is distinctly Jewish, modeled in many ways on the prayers said at the circumcision ceremony. [Some commentators] feel that this originated in Jewish circles and that they were completed with a Christian [and John the Baptizer] addition. . . .

"Like the Magnificat, this hymn of Zechariah resounds with Old Testament allusions.

"V. 68: The word 'blessed' copies the style of four of the Psalms of Praise (Pss. 34:2, 67:2, 103:1 and 113:2). The hymn blesses Yahweh for what he has achieved of salvation.

"The word 'visited' is a common biblical word meaning either favor or punishment; according to the context God cannot be present in any neutral way (see Ex. 3:16, 4:31, Lv. 18:25, Is. 10:12, and 23:16)."

5. Meditation

The saints loved to consider the many ways in which God visits His people. God is with us through His essence, presence, and power. God is immutably transcendent, and critics of Christianity, ancient and modern, view God as a distant deity who is little interested in His creation. They emphasize His tremendous majesty and distance from us here below, very far below.

But it is also of the essence of God that He is immanent in us and in the world He created. If God forgot any of His creation, no matter how minimal the time, that creation would simply cease to exist. This immanence, this all-pervasive presence of God in us, takes on the dimension of personal love through the mediation of Christ.

The presence of God can be considered in many ways

and under many aspects. He is present when we pray, and He can be seen in our neighbors. Most significant to me is His sacramental presence in the Eucharist. Through Mass and the Sacraments we have a closeness to Christ that will only be exceeded in heaven.

Creation itself is a reflection of the power of God; so is the gift of free will. In the order of grace the whole Christian dispensation represents the triumph of spirituality. God, who is omnipotent in creation, is even more wonderful in the order of redemption.

Luke 1:69

1. Text

"He has raised a horn of saving strength for us in the house of David his servant," (NAB)

"And he has established for us a saving power in the House of his servant David." (NJB)

"He has raised up a sceptre of salvation for us among the posterity of his servant David." (Knox)

"And raised up a horn of salvation for us in the house of David his servant." (Spencer)

"He has raised for us a stronghold of salvation in the house of David his servant." (Kleist)

"And has raised up a horn of salvation for us, in the house of David his servant." (CCD)

2. Old Testament roots

In Psalm 132:17 we read "In her will I make a horn to sprout forth for David." This "sprout" of David is, of course, preeminently Jesus Christ, as promised by the prophets. "Behold the days are coming, says the LORD, when I will raise up a righteous shoot to David; as King he shall reign and govern wisely, he shall do what is just and right in the land" (Jer. 23:5).

When Jeremiah speaks of the restoration of Jerusalem he promises that a Davidic king will be restored, again a type of Christ. "In those days, in that time, I will raise up for David a just shoot; he shall do what is right and just in the land" (Jer. 33:15).

King David was the great founder of the ruling house of Judah and Israel when the twelve tribes finally presented a united front after the death of King Saul. He was the youngest son of Jesse of Bethlehem, carefully chosen by God through the prophet Samuel. His genealogy is traced in Ruth 4:18ff.

In the popular mind, David was the ideal king. Anointed by the prophet after being set apart by Yahweh, he was a strong military leader, a just and caring ruler, and a musician and composer. He was also a man who sinned mightily, but repented just as mightily.

David finally captured Jerusalem and made it the capital of a unified kingdom. Because he was such a religious man, he determined to build a Temple to the Lord, but God intervened. In denying David the right to build, Yahweh promised David an eternal dynasty (see 2 Sam. 7:8-16). We see this promise fulfilled in Christ, the descendent of David.

The references to David have a special meaning for Christians who, in honoring this illustrious ancestor of the Lord, see concrete proof that God is faithful to His promises.

3. Patristic usage

St. Ignatius of Antioch: Letter to the Ephesians

"In a second letter which I intend to write to you, I shall explain more fully what I have merely touched upon — the dispensation of becoming the new man Jesus Christ, who is of the race of David according to the passion and resurrection. Come together in common, one and all without exception, in charity, in one faith, and in one Jesus Christ, who is of the race of David according to the flesh, the son of man and the Son of God, so that with undivided mind you may obey the bishop and the priests, and break one Bread, which is the medicine of immortality, and the audience against death, enabling us to live forever in Jesus Christ."

Eusebius: Ecclesiastical History

"And the prophets of succeeding times also clearly foretold Christ by name, giving testimony beforehand both to the intrigues of the people who were destined to rise against Him, and to the calling of the Gentiles through Him. At one time David says in perplexity thus: 'Why have the Gentiles raged, and the peoples devised vain things? The kings of the earth stood up, and princes met together against the Lord and His Christ,' to which he later adds in the person of Christ Himself, "The Lord has said to me: You are my Son, this day I have begotten You. Ask of me and I shall give you the Gentiles for your inheritance and the utmost parts of the earth for your possession. . . .'"

"Isaiah also teaches about this, exclaiming in one place as if from Christ Himself, 'The Spirit of the Lord is upon me. Wherefore He has anointed me to preach the Gospel to the poor, He has sent me to announce deliverance to captives, and sight to the blind.' And not only Isaiah, but also David proclaims to His Person, saying 'Your throne, O God, is forever and ever: the scepter of your kingdom is a scepter of uprightness. You have loved justice and hated iniquity: therefore, God, your God, has anointed you with their oil of gladness above your fellows.'

"Elsewhere in the Psalms, the same David makes this statement about Him, speaking clearly as follows: 'The Lord said to my Lord: Sit at my right hand until I make your enemies the footstool of your feet.' and 'From the womb before the daystar I begot You. The Lord has sworn and he will not repent,' You are a priest forever according to the order of Melchizedek.' "

4. Modern usage

Father W. J. Harrington, O.P.: St. Luke

"Zechariah, like so many others in this narrative is inspired by the Spirit of prophecy. His canticle, like the Magnificat, is a chain of Old Testament quotations and reminiscences." It gives a strong impression of having been part of an already existing psalm-prayer, well-known to Zechariah, "and put in the mouth of Zechariah to express adequately how the old priest felt on this occasion.

"As it stands, it is markedly Jewish in tone, and in the first part it praises God's great actions in the history of His people; the second part (vv. 76-79) turns to Zechariah's son and foreshadows his office and preaching.

"The hymn opens, like many of the psalms, and like later Jewish themes, in praise of God. 'Visit' is a biblical term which indicates a — generally favorable — intervention of God. In the present context the visitation and the deliverance refer to the sending of the Messiah, 'the horn of salvation' — horn is the symbol of strength — of the house of David in accordance with the prophecies (2 Sam. 7) who, in his divine strength, will save his people from their enemies.

"Then will be the overflowing of God's great mercy

86

(Mi. 7:20) when, in remembrance of his covenant (Ex. 2:24) and of his oath to Abraham (Jer. 11:5) his people can serve him, unmolested and without fear, all their days."

5. Meditation

The San Diego Zoo runs the San Diego Wild Animal Park about thirty miles north of the zoo. There, in a natural habitat of some hundreds of acres, the animals roam free in landscapes that duplicate their home ranges in Africa and Australia and Asia. The visitors sit in monorail cars far above the scene, or view it from natural points above the valleys.

It is an awesome thing to watch some of the male, honored animals in mating season doing battle. Sometimes the clash can be heard a mile away. When the biblical writers use the horn as a symbol of power and might, I envision some of these mating rituals I have witnessed. I know I wouldn't want to get caught between any of these battling males.

Biblical imagery is always intriguing since it is usually so homey, so earthy, and so expressive. Some of the translators used substitute expressions for the word "horn," but words like scepter or saving power do not present anywhere near as clear a picture.

The power of God is irresistible, but how to express it with force is a prerogative of scriptural authors, not always shared by translators. One of the reasons each chapter (verse) in this book starts out with "text," a short comparison of the translations, is to show how even a slight variation can give a new or sharper understanding of the verse or, on the other hand, make the meaning more obscure.

In a devotional work, this is not too great a hazard. In matters of more deeply theological import, it can make a great difference. Some of the older translations are not really helpful, since modern American English has grown so since they were translated. Some of the modern translations, especially the popular paraphrases such as the Good News Bible, the Cotton Patch Versions, and the Reader's Digest Bible, are definitely not helpful for any serious Bible reading. I don't like them even as introductions.

Luke 1:70

1. Text

"As he promised thrugh the mouths of his holy ones, the prophets of ancient times." (NAB)

"Just as he proclaimed, by the mouth of his holy prophets from ancient times." (NJB)

"According to the promise which he made by the lips of holy men that have been his prophets from the beginning." (Knox)

"As he hath declared through the mouth of His holy Prophets from of old." (Spencer)

"And redeemed the promise he had made through the mouth of his holy prophets of old." (Kleist)

"As he promised through the mouth of his holy ones, the prophets from of old." (CCD)

2. Old Testament roots

The theme of "prophecies" or "promises fulfilled" which runs through the Magnificat and the Benedictus, puts emphasis on the promises themselves, the prophecies that had been proclaimed and which were treasured by the Jewish people.

In the twenty-third chapter of the Prophet Jeremiah, he proclaims the glorious reign of the Messiah who will return to "shepherd" the "remnant" of the people who remain (vv. 2,3). And in verse 6, "In his days Judah shall be saved, Israel shall dwell in security. This is the name they give him: "The Lord our justice.' "

Jeremiah then goes on to condemn the false prophets who are "godless" (v. 11) and who "do unseemly deeds" (v. 13). They are like the citizens of Sodom and Gomorrah (see v. 14). "I have heard prophets who prophesy lies in my name" (v. 24). So there was the problem of sorting out true prophecy from the false and wicked. All the more treasured, then, were the prophets received by the people at the time of Mary and Zachary.

In the thirtieth chapter, Jeremiah continues his voice of emancipation, freedom, and restoration. The Chosen Race would suffer greatly for its infidelity, but the promise was sure and exact that God would be the deliverer.

"Jacob shall find rest, shall be tranquil and undisturbed" (v. 10). "For I will restore you to health; of your wounds I will heal you, says the Lord" (v. 17). "His leader shall be one of his own, and his rulers shall come from his kin" (v. 21). And the high point, "You shall be my people, and I will be your God" (v. 22).

The prophets and their words were a sacred trust, held by the Jews who were to wait, preferably patiently, until God fulfilled his promises. From the promises made to Adam and Eve in Genesis, through the further refinements found in the historical and prophetical books, the messianic threat grows ever more certain, ever more desired.

3. Patristic comment

St. Justin, Martyr: Dialogue with Trypho
"When the Magi failed to return to Herod as he had re-

89

quested, but had gone to their own country by another route, as they had been ordered, and when Joseph, Mary and the Child had already retired into Egypt, as they were divinely directed, Herod, since he had not known who the child was whom the Magi had come to worship, ordered every boy in Bethlehem without exception to be slain.

"This, too, had been foretold by Jeremiah, when the Holy Spirit spoke through him in this fashion, "A voice was heard in Rama, weeping and great lamentation; Rachel weeping for her childen, and refusing to be comforted for them, because they are not.''

''. . . And to continue in the words of Isaiah: 'Who shall declare his generation? For his life is taken from earth,' seems to indicate that He, who is said to be consigned to death by God because of the sins of the people, did not have mere human origin. . . .

"And then there are the words of David, 'In the brightness of your saints, from the womb before the daystar I begot you. The Lord has sworn and He will not repent: You are a priest forever according to the order of Melchizedek.' Do not these words signify that from ancient times God, the Father of all things, intended Him to be born again and of a human womb?''

St. Justin, Martyr: First Apology

"The prophet Isaiah spoke thus: "A star shall arise out of Jacob and a flower shall spring from the root of Jesse and in His arm nations shall trust.' Indeed, a brilliant star has arisen and a flower has sprung up from the root of Jesse, that is, Christ.

"For by God's power He was conceived by a virgin who was a descendent of Jacob, who was the father of Judah, the father of the Jewish race; and Jesse was his forefather according to this prophecy and He was the son of Jacob and Judah according to lineage.

"And again, hear how it was expressly foretold by Isaiah that He was to be born of a virgin. Here is the prophecy: 'Behold, a virgin shall conceive and bear a son, and His name shall be called Emmanuel,' that is, 'God with us.' For what man has deemed incredible and impossible, God foretold through the prophetic spirit as about to take place, so that, when they take place, they should not be denied, but delivered, because they have been foretold."

4. Modern thoughts:

Dr. Paul Heinisch: Theology of the Old Testament

Dr. Heinisch has a large section in his famous work on the fulfillment of prophecies concerning the Messianic Kingdom. In this excerpt he is discussing the cult, or worship, of the new order.

"The center of the messianic kingdom will be Zion. From there the true faith will be heralded to mankind; there the Messiah will give Himself as a sacrifice; from there the apostles will set out on their missions. Because of Zion's significance in the history of salvation, the prophets rightly designate her as the highest mountain (Is. 2:2), or as Canaan's only mountain (Zech. 14:10).

"The sanctuary of the future covenant is the temple, the levitical priesthood continues (Jer. 33:18), animals are brought as sacrifice by Jew and Gentile (Jer. 33:11, Is. 19:21) the Sabbath, New Moon and other feasts are kept sacred (Is. 66:23; Zech. 14:16-18).

"On the other hand, the ark of the covenant no longer exists (Jer. 3:16), the Aaronic priesthood is rejected (Mal. 1:10), Gentiles will serve as priests (Is. 66:21), a new sacrifice is promised wholly unlike current sacrifices (Mal. 1:11).

"Again we see the metaphorical character of prophetic terminology, the kernel of the message being simply: in

91

messianic times God will be worshipped under new cult forms (cf. Heb. 8:5; 9:23; 10:1)."

Aloys Grillmeier: Christ in the Christian Tradition

Aloys Grillmeier takes a step further in his work *Christ in the Christian Tradition*. Jesus is not only the fulfillment of the prophets; He reveals what He knews, whereas they only revealed what was told to them. Grillmeier expresses it this way:

"The climax of New Testament development of Christological thought is reached in John. His prologue to the Fourth Gospel is the most penetrating description of the career of Jesus Christ that has ever been written.

"It is not without reason that the Christological formula of John 1:14 ('And the Word was made flesh and dwelt among us') could increasingly become the most influential text in the history of dogma.

"The Johannine Christology has a dynamism all of its own. Christ appears as the definitive Word of God to man, as the unique and absolute *revealer*, transcending all prophets."

5. Meditation

They say that when we get to heaven and enjoy the beatific vision, we shall know all the "future possibles." All the answers to our "what if" questions will be answered.

"What if Adam had refused the apple; what if King Solomon had been followed to the throne by a wise and pious son; what if Jesus had been accepted by the Jews as their Lord and Messiah?" These offer intriguing avenues of thought.

But then, we return to reality. Adam did sin, the Kingdom of David was divided into two warring factions, and Jesus "came unto His own and His own received him not" (Jn 1:11). The long, dreary wait for the Messiah covered thousands of years, in which anticipation seemed endless.

This is certainly a lesson in patience and hope. Throughout those long centuries, God continually invited conversion and continually showed patience for sinners. For those many good and just men and women, it meant a lifetime of patiently waiting for the coming of Christ. What an example they are to us.

Their faith in the promises made by Yahweh and the hope kept alive through good times and bad have to be an inspiration to us in our trials and disappointments. Our faith and hope have been enlightened by the coming of Christ in history and the promise held out to us of eternal life. So much has been given to us since the promises of the Old Testament prophets have been fulfilled so generously.

Luke 1:71

1. Text

"Salvation from our enemies and from the hands of all our foes." (NAB)

"That he would save us from our enemies and from the hands of all who hate us," (MJB)

"Salvation from our enemies and from the hands of those who hate us." (Knox)

"Salvation from our foes, and from the hand of all who hate us." (Spencer)

"To grant salvation from our foes and from the hand of all that hate us." (Kleist)

"Salvation from our enemies and from the hand of all who hate us." (CCD)

2. Old Testament themes

Salvation in the Old Testament meaning centers more around actual physical deliverance from enemies than a spiritual theme. When it does have spiritual meaning, it tends to mean obedience to the Mosaic Law without deviation. The Pharisees refined it to an exact, even scrupulous, interpretation of the Law.

It remained for Christ to raise the meaning especially to the spiritual realm. St. Paul was to give us the theology of it as the freedom of the children of faith and baptism, the union of soul and God in Christ Jesus, and the elevation of the community (Church) into the body of Christ.

David, in his song of thanksgiving, cries out, "My God, my rock of refuge! My shield, the horn of my salvation, my stronghold, my refuge, my savior, from violence you keep me safe" (2 Sam. 22:3) and again, "The LORD live! . . . Extolled be my God, rock of my salvation" (v. 47).

Judith, when faced with the devastation of her people before the onslaught of the troops of Holofernes, gives this counsel: "So while we wait for the salvation that comes from him, let us call upon him to help us, and he will hear our cry if it is his good pleasure" (Jdt. 8:17).

Mordecai, facing the destruction of the people because of the machinations of Haman, prays in this way: "Gladly would I have kissed the soles of his feet for the salvation of Israel. But I acted as I did so as not to place the honor of man above that of God. I will not bow down to anyone but you, my Lord" (Est. C:6).

In the time of the Maccabees, two army leaders tried to imitate Judas Maccabee out of envy and pride, and they lost a devastating battle. The writer comments that it happened because "they did not belong to the family of those men to whom it was granted to achieve Israel's salvation." The word "salvation" in this sense is used over forty times in the Psalms, and about twenty times in the prophetic books.

3. Patristic comment

The word and idea "salvation" were frequently used in the fathers from the very beginning because salvation was so closely identified with Christ's work and the reason for conversion.

Pope St. Clement I: Letter to the Corinthians

"Let us fix our attention on the blood of Christ and recognize how precious it is to God His Father, since it was shed for our salvation and brought the gift of repentence to all the world.

"Jesus Christ is our salvation. He is the High Priest through whom we present our offerings and the helper who supports us in our weakness. Through Him our gaze penetrates the heights of heaven, and we see, as in a mirror, the most holy face of God. Through Christ the eyes of our heart are opened and our weak and clouded understanding reaches up toward the light."

St. Ignatius of Antioch: Letter to the Smyrnaeans

"By His resurrection, Christ raised up a standard over His saints and faithful ones for all time, both Jews and Gentiles, in the one body of His Church. For He endured all this for us, for our salvation; He really suffered and just as truly rose from the dead. As for myself, I am convinced that He was united with His body even after the resurrection."

St. Ambrose: Second Letter

"The Church of the Lord is built upon the rock of the Apostles among so many dangers in the world; it therefore remains unmoved. The Church's foundation is unshakeable and firm against the assaults of the raging sea. Waves lash at the Church but do not shatter it.

"Although the elements of the world constantly beat upon the Church with crashings sounds, the Church possesses the safest harbor of salvation for all in distress."

4. Modern comments

Pierre M. Benoit: Jesus and the Gospel

"The Greek word 'kerygma' is used in the New Testament to denote the first triumphant preaching that the witnesses of Christ addressed to the world to bring to its notice the 'Good News' (the meaning of the word 'evangelion,' 'Gospel') of the salvation which God had just achieved in His Son and through His Spirit."

Rudolf Schnackenburg: Christian Existence in the New Testament

"We must not overlook an aspect which is inherent in Jesus' whole message of salvation, and also underlies the demands of the Sermon on the Mount. It is: the new eschatological and primally pure morality of Jesus' disciples, the undivided surrender of God, and the unlimited love of brother become possible only by God's anticipatory love and by His present work of salvation."

Pope John XXIII: Mater et Magistra

"Mother and Teacher of all nations — such is the Catholic Church in the mind of her founder, Jesus Christ; to hold the world in an embrace of love, that even men in every age should find in her their own completeness in a higher order of living and their ultimate salvation."

Vatican II: Lumen Gentium

"Eternal salvation is open to those who, through no fault of their own, do not know Christ and His Church but seek God with a sincere heart, and under the inspiration of grace try in their lives to do His will, made known to them by the dictate of their conscience.

"Nor does Divine Providence deny the aids necessary for salvation to those who, without blame on their part, have not yet reached an explicit belief in God, but strive to lead a good life, under the influence of God's grace."

5. Meditation

Salvation has an objective side in the saving work of Jesus Christ in His Passion, Death, and Resurrection — the paschal mystery. It has a subjective side in our cooperation with the free gift of God's grace. According to the ancient axiom, "God who created us without our cooperation will not save us without our cooperation."

So, the Old Testament men and women prayed to be delivered from the armies that hedged them in on all sides. Possibly with the exception of the reign of King Solomon, there was never much of an extended peace in the Holy Land.

The New Testament figures, from the Apostles up to our time, pray for deliverance from spiritual evils as well as for world peace. In the latter case, how few have been the times when there was not war or rumor of war.

But we fight an even higher battle with the world, the flesh, and the devil in our striving to be more perfect Christians. We are called to be saints, invited to be as perfect as our heavenly Father, and our homeland is heaven.

The challenge of salvation has been widened in our faith in Christ. It's just that the stakes are higher for us, but so are the opportunities and the help of grace.

Luke 1:72

1. Text

"He has dealt mercifully with our fathers and remembered the holy covenant he made," (NAB)

"And show faithful love to our ancestors, and so keep in mind his holy covenant." (NJB)

"So he would carry out his merciful design towards our fathers, by remembering his holy covenant." (Knox)

"To show mercy to our forefathers, and to remember his holy covenant." (Spender)

"To deal in mercy with our fathers and be mindful of his holy covenant," (Kleist)

"To show mercy of our forefathers and to be mindful of his holy covenant." (CCD)

2. Old Testament themes

"Then, when their uncircumcised hearts are humbled, and they make amends for their guilt, I will remember my covenant with Jacob, my covenant with Isaac, and my covenant with Abraham; and of the land, too, I will be mindful" (Lv. 26:41-42).

"Who is there like you, the God who removes guilt and pardons sin for the remnant of his inheritance; Who does not persist in anger forever, but delights rather in clemency, and will again have compassion on us, treading underfoot our guilt? You will cast into the depths of the sea all our sins; You will show faithfulness to Jacob and grace to Abraham, as you swore to our fathers from days of old" (Mi. 7:18-20).

"He, the LORD, is our God; throughout the earth his judgments prevail. He remembers forever his covenant, which he made binding for a thousand generations — which he entered into with Abraham and by his oath to Isaac. Which he established for Jacob by statute, for Israel as an everlasting covenant" (Ps. 105:7-10).

"Let the house of Israel say, His mercy endures forever. Let the house of Aaron say, His mercy endures forever" (Ps. 118:2-3).

"Thus says the LORD, the God of Israel: Cursed be the

man who does not observe this covenant which I enjoined upon your fathers the day I brought them up out of the land of Egypt, that iron foundry, saying: Listen to my voice and do all that I command you. Then you shall be my people and I will be your God. Thus will I fulfill the oath which I swore to your fathers" (Jer. 11:3-5).

3. Patristic comment

The Fathers of the Church often treated Christ as the fulfillment of the Covenant, and saw the great biblical characters as types of Christ, the Covenant developing until its completion in the Lord.

Letter to Barnabas (Second century)

"Moses says to Joshua, the son of Nun, after giving him this name, when he sent him to explore the land, 'Take a book in your hands and write what the LORD says, that the Son of God shall in the last days tear up by the roots the whole house of Amalek' (Ex. 17:14). See again Jesus, not as son of man, but as Son of God, manifested by a type in the flesh. So, since they will say that Christ is David's son, David himself prophesies, fearing and realizing the error of sinners. 'The LORD said to my Lord: "Sit at my right hand until I make your enemies your footstool" (Ps. 110:1). . . . See how David calls Him Lord and does not say Son.' "

St. Clement of Alexandria: Christ the Educator

"Isaac is another type, too, of the Lord. He was a son, just as is the Son; he was a victim, as was the Lord, but his sacrifice was not consumated, while the Lord's was. All he did was to carry the wood of his sacrifice, just as the Lord bore the wood of the Cross.

"Isaac rejoiced for a mystical reason, to prefigure the joy with which the Lord has filled us, in saving us from destruction through His blood. Isaac did not actually suffer, not only to concede the primacy of suffering to the Word, but also to suggest, by not being slain, the divinity of the Lord."

St. Melito of Sardis: Easter Homily

"There was much proclaimed by the prophets about the mystery of the Passover: that mystery is Christ and to Him be glory for ever and ever. Amen.

". . . He was led forth like a lamb; he was slaughtered like a sheep. He ransomed us from our servitude to the world, and He had ransomed Israel from the land of Egypt; He freed us from our slavery to the devil, as he had freed Israel from the hand of Pharoah. He sealed our souls with his own Spirit, and the members of our body with His own blood.

"He is the One who covered death with shame and cast the devil into mourning. He is the One who smote sin and robbed iniquity of offspring, as Moses robbed the Egyptians of their offspring. He is the One who brought us out of slavery into freedom, out of darkness into light, out of death into life, out of tyranny into an eternal kingdom, who made us a new priesthood, a people chosen to be his own. He is the Passover that is our salvation.

"It is He who endured every kind of suffering in all those who foreshadowed Him. In Abel He was slain, in Isaac bound, in Jacob exiled, in Joseph sold, in Moses exposed to die. He was sacrificed in the Passover lamb, persecuted in David, dishonored in the prophets."

4. Modern comments

John L. McKenzie: Aspects of Old Testament Thought

"The Covenant. The relationship of Yahweh and Israel is unique in the religions of the ancient world. In other ancient religions the deity is identified either with nature or with the society that worships the deity. The relationship is, therefore, in a sense natural, since in the mind of ancient peoples both physical nature and human society are primarily data with which *man* is essentially involved.

"On the contrary, the relation of Yahweh and Israel is, like the created universe, the result of a positive action of Yahweh Himself; and the relation of Yahweh and Israel is completed by a positive response of Israel. The relation is not a given necessary component of human existence but a freely instituted community of persons. . . .

"The covenant is initiated by Yahweh through an act that is often called 'election,' especially in Deuteronomy. Israel is the people of Yahweh through the choice of Yahweh. The saving acts of Yahweh — the deliverance of the people from Egypt and the gift of the land of Canaan — establish Israel as a people and give Israel the identity and stability that the word 'people' denotes.

"The election made by Yahweh is an act of the love of Yahweh (Dt. 4:37ff.; 7:6 ff.) and is not because of the greatness or the merits of Israel (7:7, 9:4 ff.). The election of Israel imposes upon Israel the responsibility of recognizing Yahweh alone as God (4:39) and of keeping the commandments (4:40; 7:9 ff., 10:16 ff.).

"The treaty formula brings out more clearly the fact that the election of Israel is an election to responsibility and obligation, not merely to a position of privilege. The Old Testament does not conceive of election as an act of favoritism."

5. Meditation

The Church is often called the New Israel, or the New Israel of God. This is the chosen community of God, chosen by him and consecrated in the blood of Christ to form New Covenant or New Testament People of God.

It is a community bound together by religious ties, far transcending the ethnic diversity of which its members are composed. The biblical doctrine of the Mystical Body —

Christ the Head and we the members — and the equally evangelical note of Christ the Vine and we the members make this Church a definite, operable community, visible to the world.

The early Christian Church soon grew from small charismatic groups into well-organized local churches under the rule of the bishops. This is evidenced by the letters of St. Ignatius of Antioch at the end of the first Christian century, or the first decade of the second century.

When crises occurred that were beyond the power of the local bishops, they turned naturally to the Bishop of Rome, the successor of St. Peter. This also had real New Testament roots. It is the testimony of the Church Fathers and Church history, as well.

This, then, is the new covenant between us and God, in which the election has been His, the responsibilities and privilege ours.

Luke 1:73

1. Text

The oath he swore to Abraham our father he would grant us." (NAB)

"This was the oath he wrote to our father Abraham" (NJB)

"He had sworn an oath to our father Abraham" (Knox)

"The oath which he swore to Abraham our father to grant us —" (Spencer)

"Of the oath he had sworn to our father Abraham that he

would enable us —" (Kleist)

"Of the oath that he swore to Abraham our father, that he would grant us," (CCD)

2. Old Testament roots

"The LORD appeared to Abram and said, 'To your descendants I will give this land' (Gn. 12:7).

"I swear by myself, declares the LORD, that because you acted as you did in not withholding from my your beloved son, I will bless you abundantly and make your descendants as countless as the stars of the sky and the sands of the seashore; your descendants shall take possession of the gates of their enemies, and in your descendants all the nations of the earth shall find blessing — all this because you obeyed my command" (Gn. 22:16-18).

"The LORD appeared to him [Isaac] and said: 'Do not go down to Egypt, but continue to camp wherever in this land I tell you. Stay in this land, and I will be with you to bless you: for to you and your descendants I will give all these lands in fulfillment of the oath I swore to your father Abraham. I will make your descendants as numerous as the stars in the sky and give them all these lands, and in your descendants all the nations of the earth shall find blessings — this because Abraham obeyed me, keeping my mandates (my commandments, my ordinances and my instructions)' " (Gn. 26:2-5).

"ABRAHAM, father of many peoples, kept his glory without stain: He observed the precepts of the Most High, and entered into an agreement with him; In his own flesh he incised the ordinance, and when tested was found loyal. For this reason God promised him with an oath that in his descendants the nations would be blessed. That he would make him numerous as the grains of dust, and exalt his posterity like the stars; that he would give him an inheritance from sea to sea, and from the River to the ends of the earth.

103

"And for ISAAC he renewed the same promise because of Abraham, his father. The covenant with all his forebears was confirmed, and the blessing rested upon the head of JACOB" (Sir. 44:19-22).

3. Patristic theme

St. Irenaeus: Against Heresies
"And Matthew, recognizing one and the same Jesus Christ, exhibiting His generation as a man from the Virgin, even as God did promise David that He would raise up from the fruit of his body an eternal King, having made the same promise to Abraham a long time previously, says; 'The book of the generation of Jesus Christ, the son of David, the son of Abraham.'

"Then, that he might free our mind from suspicion regarding Joseph, he says 'But the birth of Christ was in this wise. When His mother was espoused to Joseph, before they came together, she was found with child of the Holy Spirit.'

"Then, when Joseph had it in contemplation to put Mary away, since she proved to be with child, Matthew tells us of the angel of God standing by him and saying: 'Fear not to take Mary as your wife, for that which is conceived in her is of the Holy Spirit. And she shall bring forth a son and you shall call His name Jesus; for He shall save His people from their sins. Now this was done that it might be fulfilled what was spoken of the Lord by the prophet: Behold, a virgin shall conceive and bring forth a son, and they shall call His name Emmanuel, which is, God with us.'

"This clearly signifies that both the promise made to the fathers had been accomplished, that the Son of God was born to a virgin, and that He, Himself, was the Christ, the Savior whom the prophets had foretold."

104

4. Modern thought

Dr. Paul Heinisch: History of the Old Testament

"With the call of Abraham (Gen. 12:1-3) a new chapter begins in the story of salvation. After the peoples of the earth had apostatized from God, God first selected a person, then his family, and finally the nation which owed its origin to him in order to accomplish His holy designs for the world's salvation.

"Home and relatives were abandoned as Abraham, the first of the patriarchs, migrated to a land unknown even by name, a land in which he would certainly lack rights and protection. His was to live and obey. In return, he was given the promise of innumerable descendants — from a sterile wife! (Gn. 11:30).

"For the nation he was destined to father should not come into existence in a purely natural manner, but through a miracle, a special act of divine favor. Again — faith.

"Moreover, God promised to bless him and make his name so famous that it would be used as a form of blessing. In messianic times all nations would participate in his good fortune, namely, the knowledge of the one true God. Material blessings were not excluded though they occupied a second rung. In this manner the promise made to Sem (Gn. 9:26) was clarified a step further.

"In the beginning of the story of salvation, the disbelief and disobedience of our first parents brought misfortune upon mankind, the faith and the obedience of Abraham were destined to be a means of divine favor and grace for all. . . .

"The patriarch's outstanding virtue was faith, faith proven by an absolute trust in the divine promises. He showed his faith at the time of his call, and later when God promised him children. Due to his faith he became the 'father of all believers' (Rom 4:11), a model for those who 'hoping against hope' rely only on God (Rom 4:18-19).

"The most exacting test of his faith occurred when he was told to sacrifice Isaac in whom the divine promises were destined to be fulfilled (Heb. 11:7). The biblical account says expressly, 'God put Abraham to the test' (Gen. 22:1). . . .

"Educated by God through spiritual trials, he slowly and laboriously attained the heights of holiness, a model for all generations."

5. Meditation

According to the philosophy of many ancient tribes, name and nature could not be separated. This was the human background to the second commandment of the Decalogue, which demanded that God's name be kept holy. Oaths, taken in the name of Yahweh, took on a special validity because of their connection with Him.

Two of the most ancient formulas for oaths were: "Truly as Yahweh lives" (1 Sm. 14:39 and many other places) and "May Yahweh do this and that to me [you]" (1 Sm. 3:17 and various places).

So, when God promised Abraham and the other patriarchs certain things under oath, it was founded on His own holiness and fidelity. This verse of the Benedictus is alive with the vibrant history of Abraham, but the importance of God's oath must not be overlooked.

A divine promise would have been ample; God displayed even more solicitude for the patriarchs by confirming His intentions in such a sacred and serious manner. This aspect of the promise was very much in the mind of Zechariah: God's very honor, His being, were involved in the fulfillment of this promise.

As a footnote, it is interesting to mention that in postexilic times, the Jews were so aware of the sacredness of

God's name that they went to great lengths to avoid it and use a substitute — LORD, the Eternal, the Highest, the Holy One, etc.

Once vowel points were invented, the Sacred Tetragrammaton YHWH was given the vowel points for Adonai (Lord) so that the reader would remember to substitute the latter word for the former. Those translators who did not understand this practice came up with the unnatural word "Jehovah."

Luke 1:74

1. Text

"That rid of fear and delivered from the enemy," (NAB)

"That he would grant us, free from fear, to be delivered from the hands of our enemies," (NJB)

"That he would enable us to live without fear, delivered from the hands of enemies," (Knox)

"That we, delivered from the hand off our foes, should serve him without fear," (Spencer)

"Rescued from the clutches of our foes — to worship him without fear," (Kleist).

"That delivered from the hand of our enemies, we should serve him without fear," (CCD)

2. Old Testament themes

In almost every book in the Old Testament, at least eighty percent of them, the concept of the enemies of God, and therefore the enemies of the chosen people of God, is an important element. The deliverance from the enemy would, therefore, be an important part of the messianic hope and a natural ingredient in the prayer of Zechariah.

The Song of Moses. "Your right hand, O LORD, magnificent in power, your right hand, O LORD, has shattered the enemy" (Ex. 15:6).

"If you heed his voice [the guardian of Israel] and carry out all I tell you, I will be an enemy to your enemies and a foe to your foes" (Ex. 23:22). "I will have the fear of me precede you, so I will throw into panic every nation you reach. I will make all your enemies turn from you in flight. . . ." (Ex. 23:27).

"And so the LORD gave Israel all the land he had sworn to their fathers he would give them. Once they had conquered and occupied it, the LORD gave them peace on every side, just as he had promised their fathers. Not one of these enemies could withstand them; the Lord brought all their enemies under their power. Not a single promise that the LORD made to the house of Israel was broken; every one was fulfilled" (Jos. 21:43-45).

The conclusion of the Canticle of Deborah: "May all your enemies perish us, O LORD! but your friends be as the sun rising in its might!" (Jgs. 5:31).

3. Patristic comment

For many of the ancient Christian writers, the physical enemies of the Old Testament were seen as symbolical of the spiritual enemies of the Church. The fear caused by the spiritual conflicts was to be resolved in the spirit of Christian love."

St. Gregory of Nyssa: On the Song of Songs

"When love has entirely cast out fear, and fear has been transformed into love, then the unity brought by our Savior will be fully realized, for all mankind

108

will be united with one another through their union with the one Supreme Good."

St. Bernard: Miscellaneous Sermons, No. Five

"The whole of the spiritual life consists of two elements. When we think of ourselves, we are perturbed and filled with a salutary sadness. When we think of the Lord, we are revived to find consolation in the joy of the Holy Spirit. From the first we derive fear and humility, and from the second hope and love."

St. Teresa of Avila: Bookmark

"Let nothing disturb you; let nothing frighten you.
All things are passing; only God does not change.
Patience wins all;
Who possesses God lacks nothing: God alone
suffices."

St. Francis de Sales: Introduction to the Devout Life

"Do not fear what may happen tomorrow. The same loving Father who cares for you today will care for you tomorrow and every day.

"Either He will shield you from suffering or He will give you the unfailing strength to bear it.

"Be at peace then, and put aside all anxious thoughts and imaginings."

4. Modern comment

Father Richard J. Foster: Psalms and Canticles of the Breviary

"God is giving to Israel an invincible Helper who will be their strength against their enemies, thus abundantly fulfilling the promises made in times past to the Prophets and Patriarchs. And what is this promised salvation? The answer is given later, toward the end of the Canticle, where we are told that the enemies are sin and Satan.

"The effects of the Savior's coming are universal, knowing no limit of space or time, so that the ancestors of the chosen race will themselves share immediately in the fruits of the redemption, entering, through the redeeming death of Christ, into full possession of their heavenly reward.

"God promised to Abraham that He would grant freedom from all fear of succumbing to the attacks of Satan, so that His faithful people would be enabled to serve Him in holiness and justice."

5. Meditation

The history of the Jewish people has been one fraught with fear of enemies. They were surrounded in Palestine with warlike tribes and nations. They had been enslaved in Egypt. Except for a few centuries under the Davidic kings, they knew very little of peace.

Their history through Christian centuries is also filled with many dark pages. The Nazi Holocaust is only one of the worst persecutions. But anti-Semitism is a reality, even today, when we are trying to be so conscious of civil rights and social justice.

We Catholics also know persecution, from the Roman Emperors to the Muslim march through the Middle East, North Africa, and Spain and the French Revolution — to mention only a few.

There has been fierce persecution in Mexico in our century, and some waves of anti-Catholicism are evidenced in our own country.

So, when Zachary mentions that human hope to be freed of fear and rid of the enemy, we can pray it with him with heartfelt meaning. When we catch bits of prejudice and bigotry in our own feelings toward others, we must take it as a warning.

Freedom for religion is one of the great centerpieces of

the American dream. There are few places in the world where the Church has the freedom it has in the United States and Canada. But the price of freedom is eternal vigilance.

All of our freedoms bring with them very serious responsibilities. License is as great an enemy of freedom as is, say, censorship. But whatever happens to restrict our freedoms should be regarded with great suspicion. It must definitely prove itself with great certitude.

In this harmless and small verse, one apt to be overlooked in the design of the whole canticle, Zachary speaks to the soul of the whole human race.

Luke 1:75

1. Text

"We should serve him devoutly and through all our days be holy in his sight." (NAB)

"To serve him in holiness and uprightness in his presence, all our days." (NJB)

"Passing all our days in holiness, and approved in his sight." (Knox)

"In holiness and justice in his presence all our days." (Spencer)

"In holiness and observance of the Law, in his presence, all our days." (Kleist)

"In holiness and justice before him all our days." (CCD)

2. Old Testament themes

"Therefore, if you hearken to my voice and keep my

111

covenant, you shall be my special possession, dearer to me than all other people, though all the earth is mine" (Ex. 19:5).

"For you are a people sacred to the LORD, your God; he has chosen you from all the nations on the face of the earth to be a people peculiarly his own" (Dt. 7:6; 14:2).

"And today the LORD is making this agreement with you; you are to be a people peculiarly his own as he promised you; and provided you keep all his commandments" (Dt. 26:18).

"Glory in his holy name, rejoice, O hearts that seek the LORD. . . . Splendor and majesty go before him, praise and joy are in his holy place. . . . Give to the LORD the glory due his name! Bring gifts and enter his presence; worship the LORD in holy attire. . . . And say, 'Save us O God our savior, gather us and deliver us from the nations, that we may give thanks to your holy name and glory in praising you'" (1 Chr. 16:10, 27, 29 35).

"Asa did what was good and pleasing to the LORD, his God. . . . He commanded Judah to seek the LORD, the God of their fathers, and to observe the law and its commands" (2 Chr. 14:1, 3).

"[Eleazar, the scribe] made up his mind in a noble manner, worthy of his years, the dignity of his advanced age, the merited distinction of his gray hair, and of the admirable life he had lived from childhood; and so he declared that above all he would be loyal to the holy laws given by God" (2 Mac. 6:23).

"[King Hezekiah] prayed to the LORD: O LORD, remember how faithfully and wholeheartedly I conduct myself in your presence, doing what was pleasing to you" (Is. 38:3).

4. Patristic comment

For the Church Fathers, as for the spiritual writers of all the Christian centuries, holiness consisted in union with Christ, the indwelling of the Holy Trinity, the life of grace. It was nourished by faith and the sacraments, and made alive through works of charity. It meant so much more than a slavish adherence to the law.

St. Irenaeus: Against Heresies

"Those then are perfect who have had the Spirit of God remaining in them, and have preserved their souls and bodies blameless, holding fast the faith of God, that is, the faith which is directed towards God, and maintaining righteous dealings with respect to their neighbors.

"Whence also he says that this handiwork is the 'temple of God,' thus declaring: 'Know you not that you are the temple of God, and that the Spirit of God dwells in you? If any man, therefore, will defile the temple of God, him will God destroy: for the temple of God is holy, which temple you are' (1 Cor. 3:16-17). Here he manifestly declares the body to be the temple in which the Spirit dwells.' ''

St. Gregory of Nyssa: On the Beatitudes

"Man is esteemed as nothing, as ashes and grass and vanity among the things that exist, yet he becomes akin to this great Majesty that can be neither seen nor heard nor thought; he is received as a son by the God of the universe.

"How can one give thanks worthily for such a gift? With what words, what thoughts that move our minds can we praise this abundance of grace?

"Man transcends his own nature, he who was subject to corruption in his mortality, becomes immune from it in his immortality, eternal from being fixed in time — in a word, a god from a man. For if he is made worthy of becoming a son of God, he will possess in himself the dignity of the Father and be made heir to the Father's goods.

113

"How munificent is this rich Lord! How generously He opens His hands wide to give us His ineffable treasures!"

St. Leo the Great: Sermon No. Twenty-one

"Let us then, dearly beloved, give thanks to God the Father, through His Son, in the Holy Spirit. Who 'for His great mercy, wherewith He has loved us,' has had pity on us; and 'when we were dead in sins, has quickened us together in Christ' (Eph. 2:5), that we might be in Him a new creation and a new production.

"Let us put off then the old man with his deeds: and having obtained a share in the birth of Christ let us renounce the works of the flesh.

"Christian, acknowledge your dignity, and becoming a partner of the divine nature, refuse to return to the old baseness by degenerate conduct. Remember the Head and the Body of which you are a member. Recollect that you were rescued from the power of darkness and brought into God's light and kingdom."

4. Modern commentary

Father Justin Taylor, S.M.: As It Was Written. . .

"Matthew, Luke, and John introduce their Gospels with an explanation of who Jesus is and where he came from. Matthew and Luke tell us that he was conceived by the Holy Spirit and born of the Virgin Mary, and they also hand on stories of the childhood of Jesus and his upbringing at Nazareth.

"These 'infancy narratives' are different in tone and style from the rest of the Gospels of Matthew and Luke. They are full of references to the Old Testament, and whole sections seem to have been written with the Jewish scriptures in mind, e.g., the annunciation (Lk. 1:26-38), which recalls the commissioning of Gideon to perform a great work on behalf of the Lord (Jgs. 6:11-24).

114

"Right from the outset Matthew and Luke want to establish Jesus as the fulfillment of the expectations of Israel. Matthew through the genealogy with which he traces Jesus' descent from Abraham and David, and Luke through three songs — of Mary (the Magnificat), of Zechariah (the Benedictus), and of Simeon (the Nunc Dimittis)."

St. Maximilian Kolbe: First Editorial
"Everyone cannot become a genius, but the path of holiness is open to all. . . .

"It is untrue that the saints were not like us. They too experienced temptations, they fell and rose again; they experienced sorrow that weakened and paralyzed them with a sense of discouragement. . . .

"They did not trust themselves but placed all their trust in God."

5. Meditation

The search for God is part of what it means to be truly human. The ancient Christian scribe put it so beautifully when he wrote: "The soul of man is naturally religious."

If this is true of natural religions, when we look at the two revealed religions, Judaism and Christianity, we see this longing to find God, to find out what He wants, and how to serve Him in a pleasing manner. In revelation we see God's response to that longing. It is a longing, as St. Augustine points out, that has been placed in us, first, by God.

Archbishop Sheen called it a sort of "divine romance," and Francis Thompson, viewing from the sinner's vantage, produced his magnificent poem "The Hound of Heaven."

The Jewish idea of holiness centered around the observance of the Law, given to Moses, the Temple worship, and the vast array of sacrifices and celebrations. It is certainly a God-centered religion, but it contains in its depths the longing for a personal Redeemer, or Messiah.

St. Paul tells us that it came in "the fullness of time" when Christ was born of a woman, born under the Law — from which He was to liberate us.

That fullness is celebrated in a hymn with text written by Father Jack May, S.J.:

> "With hearts renewed by living faith,
> We lift our thoughts in grateful prayer
> To God our gracious Father,
> Whose plan it was to make us sons
> Through His own Son's redemptive death,
> That rescued us from darkness.
> Lord, God, Savior,
> Give us strength to mold our hearts in your true
>   likeness.
> Sons and servants of our Father.

> "So rich God's grace in Jesus Christ
> That we are called as sons of light
> To bear the pledge of glory.
> Through Him in whom all fullness dwells,
> We offer God our gift of self
> In union with the Spirit.
> Lord, God, Savior,
> Give us strength to mold our hearts in your true
>   likeness.
> Sons and servants of our Father."

Luke 1:76

1. Text

"And you, O child, shall be called prophet of the Most High; For you shall go before the Lord to prepare straight paths for him," (NAB)

116

"And you, little child, you shall be called Prophet of the Most High, for you will go before the Lord to prepare a way for him," (NJB)

"And thou, my child, wilt be known for a prophet of the most High, going before the Lord to clear his way for him," (Knox)

"And thou, Child, shalt be called a prophet of the Highest; For thou shalt go before the face of the Lord to make His highways ready." (Spencer)

"And you, my little one, will be hailed 'Prophet of the Most High'; for the Lord's precursor you will be to prepare his ways;" (Kleist)

"And thou, child, shalt be called the prophet of the Most High, for thou shalt go before the face of the Lord to prepare his ways," (CCD)

2. Old Testament themes

"Comfort, give comfort to my people, says your God, speak tenderly to Jerusalem, and proclaim to her that her service is at an end, her guilt is expiated; Indeed, she has received from the hand of the LORD double for her sins.

"A voice cries out: in the desert prepare the way of the Lord! Make straight in the wasteland a highway for our God! Every valley shall be filled in, every mountain and hill shall be made low; the rugged land shall be made plain, the rough country, a broad valley.

"Then the glory of the LORD shall be revealed, and all mankind shall see it together; for the mouth of the LORD has spoken" (Is. 40:1-5).

"Lo, I am sending my messenger to prepare the way before me; And suddenly there will come to the temple the LORD whom you seek, and the messenger of the covenant whom you desire. Yes, he is coming, says the LORD of Hosts" (Mal. 3:1).

3. Patristic comments

St. Leo the Great. Letter to Flavian

"The infancy of the babe is displayed by the lowliness of the cradle; the greatness of the Almighty is proclaimed by the voices of angels. He has a man's helpless infancy in that Herod impiously tries to kill him; but He is the Lord of all, before whom the Magi kneel in supplication.

"Already, when He came to be baptized by John, the Precursor, lest it be unknown that divinity was being covered by a veil of flesh, the voice of the Father, thundering from heaven, said: "This is my beloved Son in whom I am well pleased.'"

St. Cyprian: The Good of Patience

"His every act right from the very outset of His coming is marked by an accompanying patience. From the first moment of His descent from the sublimity of heaven to earthly things, He did not disdain, though the Son of God, to put on man's flesh and, although He Himself was not a sinner, to bear the sins of others.

"Having put aside His mortality for a time, He suffered Himself to become mortal, in order that, though innocent, He might be slain for the salvation of the guilty.

"The Lord was baptized by His servant, and He, although destined to grant the remission of sins, did not Himself disdain to have His body cleansed with water of regeneration."

St. Peter Damian: On Mary

"Fortunate Elizabeth! Before her stood the Mother of the Redeemer, the Queen of Heaven; she greeted her sweetly. Even more fortunate, however, was the child she bore in her womb, for he was the first object of this royal visit. Enlightened by the Holy Spirit, he recognized the majesty of the Queen of the Angels who was greeting his mother, and it was given to him to understand the power of that greeting.''

4. Modern Commentators

Father Louis Bouyer: The Meaning of Sacred Scripture

"Prepared for by the preaching of the Baptist, that of Jesus Himself came into a milieu providentially prepared to welcome it. The whole faith of Israel had come to its maximum, condensed into what St. Luke calls 'the expectation of the consolation' (Luke 2:25).

"Those to whom Jesus spoke, those whom John had made sensitive to His Word, were those for whom the Day of Yahweh, the day on which Yahweh would enter His kingdom, the Day of the judgment when the chaff and the wheat would be forever separated on the divine threshing floor by the very breath of the Spirit, summed up in one hope the whole faith inherited from Abraham through all the prophets.

"And it is the same faith which the seer of the Apocalypse of St. John, at the summit of the revelation of the Bible, gathered up in this cry of hope for the Day of Yahweh, henceforth endowed with an unforgettable new characteristic: 'Come, Lord Jesus, come quickly' (Rev. 22:20).''

St. Alphonsus Liguori: The Glories of Mary —
The Visitation

The moment she entered that dwelling, on her first salutation, Elizabeth was filled with the Holy Spirit; St. John was cleansed from original sin and sanctified, and therefore he gave this mark of joy by leaping in his mother's womb, wishing thereby to manifest the grace he had received by means of the Blessed Virgin. . . .

119

"All these first-fruits of redemption passed through Mary as the channel through which grace was communicated to the Baptizer, the Holy Spirit of Elizabeth, the gift of prophecy to Zachary and so many other blessings to the whole house, the first graces that to our knowledge the Eternal Word had granted on earth after the Incarnation. . . .

"It is quite correct to assume that thenceforward God made Mary the universal channel, as she is called by St. Bernard: 'Such is God's will that we should have all through Mary' (in his sermon *On the Aqueduct*)."

Abbot Columba Marmion, O.S.B.: Christ in His Mysteries

"When the fullness of time comes, God crowns all His preparations by the sending of St. John the Baptizer, the last of the prophets, one whom He will render greater than Abraham, greater than Moses, greater than all, as He Himself declares, 'No one greater than John the Baptizer has been born of woman . . . yet the least in the Kingdom of God is greater than he. . .' (cf Mt 11:11).

"God wills to make St. John His herald above all the others, the very precursor of His beloved Son. . . . God is pleased to reveal the dignity of the precursor who is to bear witness that the Light and the Truth have at length appeared upon earth (Jn. 1:8).

"God wills him to be great because he has been chosen to precede so closely to One who is to come. In God's sight, the greatness of the saints is measured according to their nearness to His Son Jesus.

"See how He exalts the precursor in order to show yet once more, by the excellence of this last prophet, what is the dignity of His Word. He chooses him from an especially saintly race; an angel announces his birth, gives the name that he is to bear, and indicates the extent and greatness of his mission.

"God sanctifies him in his mother's womb; he works such miracles around his cradle that the fortunate witnesses of these marvels wonderingly ask each other: 'What do you think this child will be?' (Lk. 1:66)."

5. Meditation

In the season of Advent, when the Church prepares liturgically for the coming of Christ, three main figures predominate: Isaiah, the prophet of ancient Israel; John the Baptizer, the last prophet of the Old Testament; and Mary, the first prophet of the New Testament.

The role that John was to play as precursor, as foretold by his father Zechariah, under the prompting of the Holy Spirit, looms large in Advent, not so much for the impending Nativity of Christ, but for the role that Christ plays in the entire New Testament.

Christ fulfilled all the prophecies of the Old Testament in redeeming mankind and founding the Church, the New Israel of God. All the promises of the Old Testament are fulfilled in Him as Messiah.

John the Baptizer comes forth, an ascetic figure, from the desert, crying out, "Make straight the path of the Lord." He preaches inner conversion, a repentance for sins, and a spiritual preparation for the actual advent of the Messiah and His work.

His symbolic baptism, a faint foreshadowing of the Sacrament of Baptism, appealed to the dramatic need to do something to show repentance and an inner conversion. That the appeal was so successful was demonstrated by both St. John and St. Paul when they met followers of the Baptizer in their missionary work.

No doubt these had been zealous young Jews who, on pilgrimage to Jerusalem during John's preaching, had been baptized by him and returned to Asia Minor and Greece to spread the news of his work. Now the Apostles had to keep repeating the message that John was only the precursor, but that Jesus was the Christ, the Messiah, the longed-for fulfillment.

Many of the Apostles had been baptized by John, and it was there at the Jordan that some of them first met Christ (cf. John 1). It was there that the cry of John pointed out Jesus, "Behold, the Lamb of God. . . ."

The mighty figure of John the Baptizer is a noble link between promise and its fulfillment.

Luke 1:77

1. Text

"Giving his people a knowledge of salvation in freedom from their sins," (NAB)

"To give his people knowledge of salvation through the forgiveness of their sins." (NJB)

"Thou wilt make known to his people the salvation that is to release them from their sins." (Knox)

"To give his people knowledge of salvation through the remission of their sins." (Spencer)

"You are to impart to his people knowledge of salvation through forgiveness of their sins" (Kleist)

"To give to his people knowledge of salvation through forgiveness of their sins." (CCD)

2. Old Testament themes

The idea of being safe, or saved, through an interior, spiritual renewal is at the core of John the Baptizer's message. His work was to prepare the people for the Messiah with a spiritual message, not a triumphant warrior king who would save them from the imperial Roman legions.

Even so, it was a difficult lesson to teach to an oppressed people. The disciples and Apostles frequently had to be dissuaded from arguing over who would be the greatest in this new "Kingdom." And practically on the eve of the Passion and Crucifixion, the mother of the sons of Zebedee would ask the favor of seeing her sons, James and John, sitting at Christ's right hand in the kingdom (Mt. 20:20).

However, interior or spiritual themes are found in the Old Testament passages, such as:

"The days are coming, says the LORD, when I will make a new covenant with the house of Israel and the house of Judah. It will not be like the covenant I made with their fathers the day I took them by the hand to lead them forth from the land of Egypt; for they broke my covenant and I had to show myself their master, says the LORD.

"But this is the covenant I will make with the house of Israel after those days, says the Lord. I will place my law within them and write it upon their hearts; I will be their God and they shall be my people.

"No longer will they need to teach their friends and kinsmen how to know the LORD. All, from the least to the greatest, shall know me, says the LORD, for I will forgive their evildoing and remember their sins no more"(Jer. 31:31-34).

> "Have mercy on me, O God, in your goodness,
>   in the greatness of your compassion wipe out my
>   offense.
> Thoroughly wash me from my guilt
>   and of my sin, cleanse me. . .
> My sacrifice, O God, is a contrite spirit:
>   A heart contrite and humbled, O God, you will
>   not spurn" (Ps. 51:3-4,19).

3. Patristic comment

For the Fathers of the Church, salvation was won by the work of Christ, the God-man, and the salvation that was granted was a true freedom from sins. In their understanding of justification, man was not simply covered with the merits of Christ; man was elevated into a supernatural state of adoptive sonship, a whole new sphere of activity.

St. Clement of Rome: Letter to the Corinthians

"Let us fix our gaze on the blood of Christ and realize how precious it is to His Father, seeing that it was poured out for our salvation and brought the grace of conversion to the whole world. Let us look back over all the generations, and learn that from generation to generation the Lord has given an opportunity of repentance to all who would return to Him."

St. Augustine: Letter One Hundred Forty

"This is the grace of the New Testament, which lay hid in the Old, yet was constantly prophesied and foretold by veiled figures, so that the soul might recognize its God and be reborn to Him, by His grace. This is truly a spiritual birth, therefore not of blood, nor of the will of man, nor of the will of the flesh, but of God.

"This is called adoption. For we were something before we were the sons of God, and we received the benefit of becoming what we were not, just as the one who is adopted, before adoption, was not yet the son of the one who adopts him; still, he was one who could be adopted.

"From this begetting by grace we distinguish that son who, although He was the Son of God, came that He might become the son of man, and might give us, who were sons of man, the power to become sons of God."

St. Justin, Martyr: Dialogue with Trypho

"So that if they repent, all who wish for it can obtain mercy from God: and the Scripture foretells that they shall be blessed, saying, 'Blessed is the man to whom the Lord imputes not guilt' (Psalm 31:2); that is, having repented of his sins, that he may receive remission of them from God;"

4. Modern comments

Father Edward Schillebeeckx, O.P.: Christ, the Sacrament of Encounter with God

"Even in His humanity, Christ is the Son of God. The second person of the most holy Trinity is personally man: and this man is personally God. Therefore, Christ is God in a human way, and man in a divine way.

"As a man, He acts out His divine life in and according to His human existence. Everything He does as a man is an act of the Son of God, a divine act in a human form; an interpretation and transportation of a divine activity into a human activity.

"His human love is the human embodiment of the redeeming love of God."

Father Xavier Leon-Dufour: Life and Death in the New Testament

"Jesus claims that John had been mistreated, and He intuits that people will deal with him the same way, following the tradition of the tragic lot of the prophets.

Jesus was not only familiar with John the Baptizer; He also knew well the prophets of Israel, His people. He referred to the failure of the prophets Elijah and Elisha and even recalled what might have been a popular aphorism, 'A prophet is not without honor, except in his own country, and among his own kin, and in his own house' (Mk. 6:4)."

5. Meditation

The world says, "What price, glory!" and the Gospels tell us the cost, the price of love. It begins with joy and promise, seems to go down to defeat in the cross, and finally triumphs with the "Alleluia" song of the Easter season.

Zechariah rejoices in the coming of the Messianic age, and foresees the good news of salvation and the forgiveness of sins. What he overlooks is the fate of the prophets who spoke the good news of Yahweh.

The salvation message is glorious, even more so than the ancient priest could imagine. The paschal mystery, however, was accomplished in the blood of Christ and the agony of Calvary.

In the Incarnation a salvific plan was made manifest. The God-man brought a new plane of activity to introduce to mankind. But how high the price!

In the joy of the nativity of the precursor, there is the promise that he will share in the sufferings of Christ, "the One who is to come." It was only natural, given the history of Israel's prophets, and it was fulfilled in this final drama portrayed in the Gospels.

The glory of John the Baptizer is that he fulfilled his role so wholeheartedly, so totally.

Luke 1:78

1. Text

"All this is the work of the kindness of our God; he, the Dayspring, shall visit us in his mercy" (NAB)

"Because of the faithful love of our God in which the rising Sun has come from on high to visit us." (NJB)

"Such is the merciful kindness of our God which has bidden him come to us, like a dawning from on high" (Knox)

"In the tender mercy of our God, by which he hath visited

126

us, as the Daybreak from on high" (Spencer)

"Thanks be to the merciful heart of our God! A dawning light on high will visit us" (Kleist)

"Because the loving-kindness of our God, wherewith the Orient from on high has visited us." (CCD)

2. Old Testament themes

"I, the LORD, have called you for the victory of justice, I have grasped you by the hand; I formed you and set you as a covenant of the people, a light for the nations. To open the eyes of the blind, to bring out prisoners from confinement, and from the dungeon, those who live in darkness" (Is. 42:6-7).

"As I live, says the LORD God, I swear I take no pleasure in the death of the wicked man, but rather in the wicked man's conversion, that he may live. Turn, turn from your evil ways! Why should you die, O house of Israel?" (Ez. 33:11)

The word "Dayspring" is used only once in the New American Bible, but as is seen from the other translations, it gives the idea of a rising sun, the beauty of the dawn.

"For from the rising of the sun, even to its setting, my name is great among the nations; and everywhere they bring sacrifices to my name, and a pure offering" (Mal. 1:11).

"But for you who fear my name, there will arise the sun of justice with its healing rays; and you will gambol like calves out of the stall" (Mal. 3:20).

"God the LORD has spoken and summoned the earth, from the rising of the sun to its setting. From Zion, perfect in beauty, God shines forth" (Ps. 50:1-2).

"Now will I recall God's works; what I have seen I will describe. At God's word were his works brought into being; they do his will as he has ordained for them. As the rising sun is clear to all, so the glory of the LORD fills all his works" (Sir. 42:15-16).

"May all your enemies perish thus, O LORD! But your friends be as the sun rising in its might!" (Jgs. 5:31).

3. Patristic comment

From the earliest Christian times, the interplay between the sun as a powerful ruling force in nature (worshiped at times by pagans) and Jesus, the Son of God, Savior of the world, captured the imagination of writers. In English, of course, with the words sounding the same, the play on words was even stronger.

But Jesus as savior was, for many of the Fathers, the rising sun of our faith, the source of our bright hope, and the inspiration of our charity. St. Bernard was particularly fond of the notion of "savior" as applied to Christ.

St. Bernard: On the Circumcision

"The circumcision proves, beyond a shadow of doubt, the fact of His humanity; the name indicates the majesty of His glory. He was circumcised because He was truly a son of Abraham; He was called Jesus, the name that is above all names, because He was truly the Son of God.

"Unlike those before Him who had the same name as a mere title, Jesus bears His name as the truth which before had only been symbolized. Heaven itself had given Him this name, for the Evangelist says it is the name 'which was used by the angel just before He was conceived in the womb' (Lk 2:21).

"Note the depth of this thought. He is called Jesus after His birth by men, but the angel acknowledged this even before His conception. He is the Savior of both angels and men; of men by reason of the Incarnation; of angels, from the time of their creation.

"What had been symbolized by the prophets is now

128

made manifest by the Gospels — the Savior is incarnate."

Letter to Barnabas (second century)

"Since then he has renewed us by the forgiveness of sins. He made us another product, and we have the souls of children, as though He were creating us again."

St. Maximus, the Confessor: Letter Eleven

"God's will is to save us, and nothing pleases him more than our coming back to him with true repentance. The heralds of truth and the ministers of divine grace have told us this from the beginning, repeating it in every age.

"Indeed, God's desire for our salvation is the primary and preeminent sign of his infinite goodness. It was precisely in order to show that there is nothing closer to God's heart that the divine Word of God the Father, with untold condescension, lived among us in the flesh and did, suffered and said all that was necessary to reconcile us to God the Father when we were at enmity with Him, and to restore us to the life of blessedness from which we had been exiled."

4. Modern comment

The loving kindness shown to us is the salvation poured out for us and on us in Christ the Savior.

Dietrich von Hildebrand: Transformation in Christ

"The readiness to change is an essential aspect of the Christian's basic relation with God; it forms the core of our response to the merciful love of God which bends down upon us: 'With eternal charity has God loved us; so He has drawn us lifted from the earth to His merciful Heart' (Antiphon: Feast of the Sacred Heart).

"To us all has the inexorable yet beatifying call of Christ been addressed, 'Come, follow Me,' Nor do we follow it unless, relinquishing everything we say with St. Paul, 'Lord, what would You have me do?' (Acts 9:6).

Rudolf Schnackenburg: Christian Existence in the New Testament

"We must not overlook an aspect which is inherent in Jesus' whole message of salvation, and which also underlies the demands of the Sermon on the Mount. It is this: the new eschatological and primally pure morality of Jesus' disciples, the undivided surrender of God, and the unlimited love of brother which became possible only by God's anticipatory love and by His present work of salvation.

"Perfection is not only a requirement, it is a gift as well: it is man's answer to God's work which makes man capable of perfection."

Pope John XXIII: Mater et Magistra

"Mother and teacher of all nations — such is the Catholic Church in the mind of her Founder, Jesus Christ; to hold the world in an embrace of love, that even men in every age should find in her their own completeness in a higher order of living and their ultimate salvation.

"She is the pillar and the ground of truth. To her her holy Founder entrusted the twofold task of giving life to her children and of teaching and guiding them, both as individuals and as nations, with maternal care. Great is their dignity, a dignity she has always guarded most zealously and held in the highest esteem."

The richness of God's grace in Jesus Christ, the kindness of God which makes it available to the faithful, must not blind us to thoughts about the salvation of those who do not know Christ:

Vatican II: Lumen Gentium

Eternal salvation is open to those who, through no fault of their own, do not know Christ and His Church but seek God with a sincere heart, and under the inspiration of grace try in their lives to do His will, made known to them by the dictate of their conscience. Nor does Divine Providence deny the aids necessary for salvation to those who, without blame on their part, have not yet reached an explicit belief in God, but strive to lead a good life, under the influence of God's grace."

5. Meditation

This is one of the easiest verses in the Benedictus to apply to the Christian way of life. The "goodness and kindness" of God are so apparent to us in the Incarnation and the Nativity of Christ that it is difficult to find new ways of expressing the facts. Only the saints, poets, and artists can even try to do so.

From Cana of Galilee through Calvary, Easter, and Pentecost, we witness the Divine Providence at work "in the fullness of time." Since it is axiomatic that the Christian is a man or woman of prayer, we find practical evidence of God's goodness to us as individuals. In each sacrament, and in the Church itself, we find true encounters with Christ.

In Sacred Scripture we find intellectual nourishment for the soul as well. Christ, the Light of the world, brings the dawn and day of spiritual maturity to those who have the insight to treasure these books. What a richness we find in our Catholic faith!

Wise, indeed, is that person who takes the time to count the blessings in the Christian calling.

Luke 1:79

1. Text

"To shine on those who sit in darkness and in the shadow of death, to guide our feet into the way of peace." (NAB)

"To give life to those who live in darkness and the shadow of death, and to guide our feet into the way of peace." (NJB)

"To give light to those who live in darkness, in the shadow of death, and to guide our feet into the way of peace." (Knox)

"To shine on those who sit in darkness and in the shade of death; to guide our feet into the path of peace." (Spencer)

"To shine upon those who sit in darkness and in the shadowland of death, and guide our feet into the path of peace." (Kleist)

"To shine on those who sit in darkness and in the shadow of death, and to guide our feet into the way of peace." (CCD)

2. Old Testament themes

"The people who walked in darkness have seen a great light; upon those who dwelt in the land of gloom a light has shone. You have brought them abundant joy and great rejoicing, as they rejoice before you as at the harvest, as men make merry when dividing spoils" (Is. 9:1-2).

"Then your light shall break forth like the dawn and your wound shall quickly be healed; your vindication shall go before you, and the glory of the LORD shall be your rear guard" (Is. 58:8).

"Rise up in splendor! Your light has come, the glory of the LORD shines upon you. See, darkness covers the earth and thick clouds cover the peoples; but upon you the LORD shines and over you appears his glory. Nations shall walk by your light and kings by your shining radiance" (Is. 60:1-3).

"They cried to the Lord in their distress; from their

straits he rescued them. And he led them forth from darkness and gloom and broke their bonds asunder" (Ps. 107:13-14).

"I will make a covenant of peace with them, and rid the country of ravenous beasts, that they may dwell securely in the desert and sleep in the forests. I will place them about my hill, sending rain in due season, rains that shall be a blessing to them. The trees of the field shall bear their fruits and the land its crops, and they shall dwell securely on their own soil. Thus they shall know that I am the Lord, when I break the bonds of their yoke and free them from the power of those who enslaved them" (Ez. 34:25-27).

3. Patristic themes

The ancient writings quickly made the crossover from physical darkness to the darkness of sin, with the way to peace being acceptance of the saving grace of Christ, and His merciful love for us sinners.

St. Basil: Homily on Psalm Thirty-three

" 'Turn away from evil and do good, seek after peace and pursue it' (Ps. 33:15).

"Concerning this peace the Lord said, 'Peace I leave with you, my peace I give to you; not as the world gives peace do I give to you' (Jn. 14:27). Seek therefore after the peace of the Lord and pursue it. And you will not pursue it otherwise than by running toward the goal, to the prize of the heavenly calling. For the true peace is from above.

"Yet, as long as we are bound to the flesh, we are yoked to many things which also trouble us. Seek, then, after a peace, a release from the troubles of this world; possess a calm mind, a tranquil and unconfused state of soul, which is neither agitated by the passions nor drawn aside by false doctrines that challenge by their persuasiveness to assent, in order that you may obtain 'the peace of God which surpasses all understanding, and which guards your heart.'

"He who seeks after peace seeks Christ because He Himself is our peace who has made us into the new man, making peace through the blood of His cross, whether on earth or in the heavens."

St. Augustine: The City of God

"The mediator between men and God was to possess a passing morality and an enduring beatitude, so that by means of a passing element, He might be conformed to men who are mortal and then transport them from death to that which endures. . . .

"The fact that He is the Word is not the reason why He is the mediator; for certainly the Word at the summit of immortality and the apex of beatitude is far removed from miserable mortals. Rather He is the mediator because He is man, and as man shows us that to attain that supreme Good, blessed and beatific, we need not seek others mediators to serve like rungs on a ladder of ascent.

"For the blessed God who makes us blessed, by deigning to share our humanity, showed us the shortest way to sharing His divinity. Freeing us from mortality and misery, He leads us, not to the immortal, blessed angels to become immortal and blessed by sharing their nature, but to that Trinity in communion with which even the angels are blessed.

When, then, in order to be a mediator, He willed to take the nature of a slave below the angels, He remained in the form of God above the angels, being at the same time the way of life on earth and life itself in heaven."

Pope St. Leo the Great: Letter to Emperor Leo

"The outpouring of Christ's blood for sinners was so rich in value that, if all the enslaved believed in the Redeemer, none of them would be held by the chains of the devil. Since those born under the sentence of original sin have received the power of rebirth unto justification, the gift of freedom became stronger than the debt of slavery. . . .

"For among the sons of men only one stood out, our Lord Jesus Christ, who was truly the spotless Lamb, in whose Person all were crucified, all died, all were buried, all were raised from the dead."

St. Athanasius: On the Incarnation, No. Eight

"This is the reason why the Word assumed a body that could die: this was the way in which the Word was to restore mankind to immortality, after it had fallen into corruption, and summon it back from death to life.

"He utterly destroyed the power death had against mankind, as fire consumes chaff, by means of the body He had taken and the grace of the Resurrection."

4. Modern commentators

Father W. J. Harrington, O.P.: St. Luke

(Commenting on the first chapter of Luke, vv. 76-77.) "These verses, addressed to the infant John, point to his vocation of Prophet and Precursor. It suggests the assimilation of Jesus to Yahweh and so his transcendence. John will declare, going beyond the perspective of the first part, that true salvation consists in the forgiveness of sins. Salvation in terms of remission of sins is a favorite theme of Luke.

"Vv. 78-79. This indicates that the true salvation is the fruit of the loving mercy of God, and will be brought from on high by the 'rising Sun i.e., the Messiah or messianic age. The shadow of death is thick darkness, the darkness of sin which will be dissipated by the messianic light. That same Sun will guide men along the right way of true peace, the faithful service of God."

Father Carroll Stuhlmueller, C.P.: The Gospel According to Luke

(Commenting on the first chapter of Luke, vv. 76-79.) "The second stanza sees the hopes of the Old Testament Fathers at the dawn of fulfilment through the intervention of Zechariah's son. The child will be Elijah, whose coming before the End-time was announced by Malachi, 3:1,23f. So close is this verse to the Old Testament expectation voiced by Malachi and Isaiah (Dt.) that no mention is made of a Messiah: God will wondrously intervene among His people.

"The Christian people saw a new meaning in both Malachi and this canticle, when God intervened to save His people in Jesus. The Messiah is hinted at in a mysterious name, 'shoot,' or 'sprout' or the 'rising sun (or star),' in verse 78. Like the terms 'servant' and 'son of man' this Messianic title quickly passed out of use in the Christian community.

"In verse 79, 'in darkness and the shadow of death,' is a combination from Is. 9:1-2 and Is. 42:7, as found in the Septuagint version. When the darkness of sin and the need is blackest, men will understand that God alone is the Savior."

5. Meditation

In this century, which has witnessed crisis after crisis, wars, police actions, genocide, depressions, and atom bombs, we must cry out for peace. To whom shall we turn, if not to God?

The critics tell us that we are in a post-Christian age, and that leaves us in a position of no hope. The physical scientists and the social scientists are powerless to save us or effect peace in the world. Political leaders have no clear-cut set of plans, and the military would spend us to death.

We desperately need to pay attention to this song of

Zechariah's. Our world needs another John the Precursor to turn our thoughts back to God and His Christ. Mankind, with its back to the wall, having tried every conceivable substitute for peace, must once again rediscover Christ.

We Christians, dedicated priests, Religious, and laity, must be a clear channel through which the message of Christ sounds, loud and strong. Our prayer, at the end of the twentieth century must be that of St. Francis: "Make me, O Lord, an instrument of Your peace!"

Appendix B
The *Nunc Dimittis*

Luke 2:29-32

1. Text

"Now, Master, you can dismiss your servant in peace; you have fulfilled your word. For my eyes have witnessed your saving deed displayed for all the peoples to see: a revealing light to the Gentiles, the glory of your people Israel." (NAB)

"Now, Master, you are letting your servant go in peace as you promised; for my eyes have seen the salvation which you have made ready in the sight of the nations; a light of revelation for the gentiles and glory for your people Israel." (NJB)

"Ruler of all, now dost thou let thy servant go in peace, according to thy word; for my own eyes have seen that saving power for thine which thou has prepared in the sight of all nations. This is the light which shall give revelation to the Gentiles, this is the glory of thy people Israel." (Knox)

"Now Thou dost release Thy servant, O Master according to Thy word, in peace! Because mine eyes have seen Thy salvation, which Thou hast made ready in the sight of all peoples — a Light of Revelation to the Gentiles, and the glory of Thy people Israel." (Spencer)

"Now you may release your bondsman, O Master, according to your promise, in peace! For my eyes have looked upon the salvation which you have prepared for all the nations to behold, a Light to illumine the Gentiles, a Glory to grace your people Israel." (Kleist)

Now thou dost dismiss thy servant, O Lord, according to thy word, in peace; because my eyes have seen thy salvation, which thou has prepared before the face of all peoples: A light of revelation to the Gentiles, and a glory for thy people Israel." (CCD)

2. Old Testament sources

Simeon was probably of the Sadducee group, and it must have been painful to him to see the gradual loss of faith in that priestly caste. He was in the Temple when Mary and Joseph came to present and redeem Jesus, according to the ritual of the Mosaic law (Lv. 12:2-4; Nm. 18:15-16).

Mary and Joseph used the sacrifice prescribed for the poor, two turtle doves or two pigeons, one for a sacrifice of praise, the other a sin offering (Ex. 13:1-16). Inspired by the Holy Spirit, Simeon not only prays the prayer we now use in the Liturgy of the Hours at night prayer, the *Nunc Dimittis*; he also is inspired to prophesy to Mary that she will be the Woman of Sorrows, with the sword that will pierce her heart (see vv. 34-35).

There was also a prophetess who came in to share in the work. Only eight women are referred to in the Old Testament as prophetesses: Sarah, Miriam, (Ex. 15:20), Deborah (Jgs. 4:4), Hannah, the mother of Samuel (1 Sm. 2:1), Abigail, the wife of David (1 Sm. 25:32), Huldah (2 Kgs. 22:14), and Esther. The wife of Isaiah is also mentioned as a prophetess. The Anna of 2 Lk. 36-38 joins this illustrious and exclusive group.

The prayer that Luke attributes to Simeon is almost a

direct reflection of the words of Isaiah and entirely in keeping with what we can know about Simeon. It is certainly in keeping with our theme of "prophecies fulfilled."

"I, the LORD, have called you for the victory of justice, I have grasped you by the hand; I formed you and set you as a covenant of the people, a light for the nations" (Is. 42:6).

"I am bringing on my justice, it is not far off, my salvation shall not carry; I will put salvation within Zion, and give to Israel my glory" (Is. 46:13).

"It is too little, he says, for you to be my servant, to raise up the tribes of Jacob, and restore the survivors of Israel; I will make you a light to the nations, that my salvation may reach to the ends of the earth" (Is. 49:6).

"The LORD has bared his holy arm in the sight of all the nations; all the ends of the earth will behold the salvation of our God" (Is. 52:10).

3. Patristic treatment

St. Augustine: Thirteenth Sermon for the Season

"While still being carried in the womb, He is saluted by John the Baptizer, still in his mother's womb. Presented in the Temple, He is acknowledged by Simeon, an old man who was well-known, aged, proved, crowned. Simeon first recognized Him, then adored Him, and then exclaimed, 'Now dismiss Your servant in peace, O Lord, for I have seen Your gift of salvation, personally.

"Simeon's exit from the world was delayed so that he might see Him born who had founded the world. The ancient one knew the Infant; in this Child he became a child again. Filled as he was with faith, he was renewed in his old age.

"Simeon, the old man, carries the infant Christ; Christ the infant rules the old man, Simeon. He had been told by the Lord that he would not taste death until he had seen

140

Christ, the Lord. Christ was born, and the desire, so old in this man's yearning, is fulfilled in his old age. He who found a world growing old comes to an old man."

St. Ambrose: Second Book of Commentaries on Luke

"And there was a just man in Jerusalem, named Simeon, devoutly awaiting the consolation of Israel. Testimony to the birth of the Lord is given not only by angels, prophets, and shepherds, but also by just men and elders. All ages and both sexes, as well as miraculous events, strengthen our faith. . . .

"He received Him in his embrace and, blessing God, he said, 'Now dismiss your servant in peace, O Lord, according to Your word.' See, here, a just man imprisoned in the body, but desiring to be released that he may be with Christ. He knows that it is a great favor to be released from this life in order to be with Christ.

"Let anyone who wishes to share this favor come to the Temple, come to Jerusalem, await Christ, receive the Word of God in his arms and embrace Him by good works, as the strong arms of faith. Then he, too will be dismissed, not that he will never see death, but because he has seen Life."

St. Bernard: On the Twelve Stars

"The martyrdom of the Virgin, begun in the prophecy of Simeon, reaches its height in the history of the Passion of the Lord. To the infant Jesus, Simeon had said, "This Child is to be a sign which will be contradicted.' To the Mother he had said, 'A sword shall pierce your very soul.'

"O truly Blessed Mother, the sword has pierced. The only way it could cut was to see the piercing of your divine Son. After He had breathed His last, when the cruel sword could not touch His Spirit as it passed through His side, surely it pierced your own soul.

"His soul was no longer there, but yours did not draw back. Surely it received the wound. We call you more than

141

a martyr because the passion of sense pain was exceeded by the compassion of love."

4. Modern authors

Father John P. Kealy, C.S.Sp.: Luke's Gospel Today

(The Presentation of Jesus, Luke 2:22-40) "Here, the Law, the prophets, and the Temple provide a background as the future career and mission of Jesus is predicted. The Mosaic Law commanded three ceremonies to follow the birth of a firstborn male child: circumcision, redemption, purification (see Lv. 12:1ff; Ex. 13:1ff; Nm. 18:15).

"Here Luke emphasizes some five times the Law and the fact that Jesus' parents, like John's, were faithful people who carefully carried out all its commandments. Also, Luke shows us here Jesus coming (on his way home to Nazareth) to Jerusalem for the first time.

"We have no angel's revelation, but Jesus is welcomed by the best of Judaism (not priests!). In a son and daughter of Israel who are waiting for its consolation, the spirit of prophecy comes alive as foretold by Joel (Jl. 3:2) about the last days which have *now* arrived. Two further clarifications about the mission of Jesus are also made here.

"The universal aspect of the worldwide mission to the Gentiles (from Jerusalem) is mentioned for the first time. Secondly, in contrast to the joy of the announcement and birth stories, a stark note of opposition, contradiction, and suffering is struck as Jesus is recognized as the Suffering Servant of Isaiah."

A. Plummer: The Gospel According to St. Luke

"In its suppressed rapture and vivid intensity this canticle equals the most beautiful of the Psalms. Since the fifth century it has been used in the evening services of the Church and has often been the hymn of dying saints. It is the sweetest and most solemn of all the canticles."

Father J. Lebreton, S.J.: The Life and Teaching of Jesus
  Christ Our Lord

(On the three canticles in St. Luke:) "These wide perspectives of glory and light were truly prophetic, but how many years and centuries were to pass before the nations would all be brought within the circle of God's light. Such joy and triumphant assurance are more in keeping with the dawn of Christianity than with the period when the Gospel was written and when Israel's glory seemed so far away. This fact, with many others, confirms the antiquity of these three hymns, piously preserved and transcribed by St. Luke."

Jordan, Clarence: The Cotton Patch Version of Luke
  and Acts (A Paraphrase)

  "Now let your servant, Almighty Master,
  Slip quietly away in peace, as you've said.
  For these eyes of mine have seen your deliverance
  Which you have made possible for *all* of the people.
  It's a light to illuminate the problem of races,
  A light to bring honor to your faithful disciples."

5. Meditation:

The Nunc Dimittis gives us a very intimate glance into the spiritual life and longing of a devout Jew at the time of Christ. What faith it demonstrates in the prophecies, what longing for their fulfillment, what exultation in their presence!

Christians have taken it over with an eagerness that makes it a daily part of the Evening Prayer in the Liturgy of the Hours (formerly Compline in the Divine Office, the Breviary) and a part of the prayers for the dying.

Simeon's words expressed his solemn joy at the fact that God had fulfilled the promise given to him, personally, as well as to Israel. The Messiah had arrived in the world;

143

the messianic age had begun. But Simeon didn't even suspect the fullness, the richness of the fact.

Simeon probably shared the popular notion of a Messiah who would save the nation from foreign oppressors, in this case the Romans. Even the Apostles had to be weaned away from that idea. Christ had to reveal to us the true nature of the Messiah sent by God.

That Christ was God, that Emmanuel, "God-with-us," was a literal fact — that was left for Christians to proclaim. Glorying in that knowledge, the Nunc Dimittis takes on a whole new spirituality.

What the patriarchs and prophets could only know dimly, and in vision, was the rich treasure of the Church, a possessed and shared fact. The Light to the Gentiles, the Glory of Israel, was the Son of God Incarnate. His entrance into history was a glorious fact; His establishment of the Church was a monument to His mercy, and His personal union with the individual Christian is a fact unique and without equal.

If Simeon spoke for the soul of every pious Jew, his prayer is for Everyman, the Christian.

Acknowledgements:

Basic Bible text from the *New American Bible*, St. Anthony Guild Edition.
> This text was used because it is so familiar to Americans from its use on Sundays. (NAB)

Quotations from:
> *The New Testament*, Confraternity of Christian Doctrine, St. Anthony Guild Press. (CCD)
>
> *The New Testament*, Father James Kleist, S.J., Bruce. (Kleist)
>
> *The New Testament*, Msgr. Ronald Knox, Sheed & Ward. (Knox)
>
> *The New Jerusalem Bible*, Doubleday. (NJB)
>
> *The New Testament*, Father Francis A. Spencer, O.P., Macmillan (Spencer)
>
> *Novum Testamentum, Graece et Latine*, Augustinus Merk, S.J. (Merk)

Also consulted:
> *The Holy Bible*, Revised Standard. The Liturgical Press.
>
> *The New English Bible*, Oxford.
>
> *The New Catholic Bible*. Our Sunday Visitor.
>
> *The New Testament*, Westminster Version. Lattey. Longmans.
>
> *The New Testament*, Modern English, Phillips. Macmillan.
>
> *The Holy Bible*, Douay Version. P.J. Kenedy & Sons.
>
> *The Holy Bible*, King James Version, The Gideons.

Excerpts of commentary were taken principally from my own, previously published anthologies. They were divided into "patristic" and "modern," more by arbitrary decision than exact historical age.

Commentary sources:

A Voice Said Ave! St. Paul Editions

Jesus, Lord! St. Paul Editions

Marmion: Fire of Love. Herder.

The Book of Catholic Wisdom. Our Sunday Visitor Press

The Catholic Tradition (14 vols.). Consortium Press

Civil Rights: A Source Book. St. Paul Editions

Prayers for the Third Age. Our Sunday Visitor Press.

Reference works:

The Jerome Biblical Commentary. Prentice-Hall

The New Catholic Commentary. Nelson

Nelson's Concordance. The Liturgical Press

McKenzie, John, *Dictionary of the Bible*. Bruce

Harper's Bible Dictionary. Harper & Row.

New Catholic Encyclopedia — The Catholic University of America

Other excerpts are acknowledged from the following sources:

Heinisch, Paul, *Theology of the Old Testament*, Liturgical Press.

————, *History of the Old Testament*, Liturgical Press.

Willis, John, *Teachings of the Church Fathers*, Palm Publishers.

Foster, Richard, *Psalms and Canticles of the Breviary*, Newman.

Taylor, Justin, *As It Was Written*, Paulist Press.

Marmion, Columba, *Christ in His Mysteries*, Herder.

O'Connell, J., *Favorite Newman Sermons*, America

Ffinch, Michael, *G.K. Chesterton*, Harper & Row.

Buddy, Charles F., *Going, Therefore, Teach. . .* U.S.D. Press

Kealy, John, *Luke's Gospel Today*, Dimension.

Maestri, William, *Mary: Model of Justice*, Alba House.

Bouyer, Louis, *The Meaning of Sacred Scripture*, Desclée.

St. Alphonsus Liguori, *The Glories of Mary*, Redemptorist.

Leon-Defour, Xavier, *Life and Death in the New Testament*, Harper & Row.

Jordan, Clarence, *Cotton Patch Version of Luke*, Association Press.

Moran, Patrick, *Day by Day with Mary*, Our Sunday Visitor.

Coughlin, Charles E., "By the Sweat of Thy Brow," Radio League.

Index

David (King) — 12, 21, 58, 65, 79, 85-86, 90, 92, 99, 100, 104, 115.
Deborah — 108, 139.
Dei Verbum — 71.

Egypt — 41, 52, 90, 99, 100, 110.
Elijah — 125, 136.
Elisha — 136.
Elizabeth — 15, 17, 18, 19, 26, 53-54, 55, 67, 76, 77, 118-119, 120.
Emmanuel — 91, 104, 144.
Epiphanius, St., — 20, 72
Esther — 28, 40, 94, 139.
Eucharist — 83, 85.
Eusebius — 85-86.
Eve — 17, 29, 42-43, 48, 65, 72, 89.
Exodus — 33, 57, 61.
Ezekiel — 30, 127, 133.

faith — 38-39, 104-105.
fear — 33-34.
Ffinch, Michael — 48-49.
Fiat — 33.
Foster, Richard J. — 109-110.
Francis de Sales, St. — 109.
Francis of Assisi, St. — 137.

Gabriel, St. — 15, 17, 19, 46, 49, 68, 76, 128.
Genesis — 28, 62, 63, 89.
Gerson, Jean — 18.
Gideon — 114.

Graystone, G. — 55-567.
Gregory of Nyssa, St. — 108-109, 113-114.
Grillmeier, Aloys — 92.

Hagar — 24, 63.
Haman — 40, 94.
Harrington, W.J. — 26, 135.
Heinisch, Paul — 91-92, 105-106.
High Priest — 35.
holiness — 113, 115.
Holy Spirit — 22, 26, 27, 31, 43, 47, 53, 78, 104, 109, 113, 114, 118-119.
Holy Trinity — 31, 38, 113, 125.
horn — 87.
Huldah — 139.

Ignatius of Antioch, St. — 85, 95, 102.
Immaculate Conception — 50.
Incarnation — 18, 22, 26, 33, 67, 120, 126, 131, 135, 144.
infancy — 114-115, 118.
Irenaeus, St. — 72, 104, 113.
Isaac — 63, 66, 98, 99, 103, 104.
Isaiah — 16, 21, 57, 67, 80, 90, 91, 104, 117, 121, 127, 132, 136, 140, 142.
Ishmael — 24, 63.
Israel — 18, 28, 31-32, 59, 61, 84, 94, 98, 100-101, 108, 119, 139, 140.

Jacob — 52, 66, 89, 90, 100.

151

153

Saul — 84.

savior — 20-21, 80, 109.

Schillebeeckx, Edward — 125.

Schnackenburg, Rudolf — 96, 130.

sex — 31-32, 53-54, 141.

Sheen, Fulton — 32, 115.

Simeon — 139-140, 143-144.

Sixtus IV, Pope — 50.

Sodom, Gomorrah — 89.

Solomon — 30, 79, 97.

Sophronius, St. — 25.

Stalin — 50.

Star of the Sea — 12-13.

Stuhlmueller, Carroll — 38-39, 82, 136.

Taylor, Justin — 114-115.

Te Deum — 31.

Temple — 31, 113, 139-142.

temptation — 13.

Teresa of Avila, St. — 109.

Tertullian — 72.

Theotokos — 18.

Thomas Aquinas, St. — 59, 76.

Thompson, Francis — 115.

Vatican II — 96, 130-131.

Vespers — 70.

Virgin (Blessed) — 21, 28, 30, 36, 41-42, 47, 53, 91, 104, 114.

Visitation — 16-17, 18, 22, 69-70, 82, 96.

Von Hildebrand, Dietrich — 129.

Wansbrough, Henry — 22.

Wisdom — 16, 31.

women — 23-24, 30-31, 60.

Word, *see* Jesus Christ.

Yahweh — 18, 21, 43, 66, 73, 84, 93, 100-101, 106, 119, 135.

Zachary (Zechariah) — 9, 67, 76, 79, 81, 82, 86, 106, 111, 121, 126, 135.

Zion (Sion) — 18, 55, 91.